TRADITIONAL WOODLAND CRAFTS

A PRACTICAL GUIDE

Feb 2001

Have a great B'in
love, now and also

Jo xxx
x.

Traditional Woodland Crafts

A Practical Guide

— ◆ —

RAYMOND TABOR

B. T. BATSFORD LTD · LONDON

For Richard – the next woodman

First published 1994
Reprinted 1996, 1997, 2000

Typeset by Graphicraft Typesetters Ltd.,
Hong Kong
and printed in Great Britain by
Butler & Tanner Ltd, Frome

Published by
B. T. Batsford Ltd
9 Blenheim Court
Brewery Road
London N7 9NT

A member of the Chrysalis Group plc

A catalogue record for this book is available
from the British Library

ISBN   0 7134 7500 5

Contents

ACKNOWLEDGEMENTS

My greatest debt is to Cyril Mummery: he it was who introduced me to the coppice crafts, thus starting a lifetime passion, and who introduced me to men of Kent who still love and work their woodlands. He also read the manuscript and made many valuable comments.

Almost every item in this book has come to mind as a result of watching, listening and talking to countless people whose lives revolve in some way around woodlands or tools. It is not possible to acknowledge each one individually, but I must record my special thanks for their unstinting advice and genuine friendship to Noel Cullum – Suffolk rake-maker and woodman; the late Frank Bird – Suffolk hurdlemaker; Charles West – Dorset hurdle and broche maker; Sidney Lukehurst – Kent hurdle and spile maker; and Barry Gladwell – Suffolk master thatcher.

I received invaluable help from Dr. Ted Collins of the Institute of Agricultural History for discussion on the woodland trades as well as access to the Institute's unrivalled collection of tools and photographs, and from Dr. Oliver Rackham of Cambridge for helpful comments and visits to Shadwell Wood. My long sessions with Fred Hams helped me to understand edge tools better, whilst those tools made for me by Alec Morris in Devon and Andrew Breese in Sussex proved essential to practising some of the crafts. I am grateful to Will Wall, archaeologist from Suffolk, for demonstrating modern methods of making charcoal.

My special thanks go to the Essex Wildlife Trust for their support of Cyril and myself whilst managing their beautiful Shadwell Wood reserve for the past 20 years; I hope its recent designation as a Site of Special Scientific Interest reflects in part the way we have done it.

For the photographs I am indebted to the Institute of Agricultural History and Museum of English Rural Life, University of Reading for figures 33, 35, 45, 54, 69, 107, 118, 121, 124, 131, 134, 159, 161, 166, 168; Angela Hampton for figure 174; and my publishers for figures 84, 148 and 151. The remainder are my own.

Finally I must thank my family for putting up with the inconveniences that resulted from my writing this book, and especially my wife, Judith, for typing the manuscript again and again.

Ray Tabor
Hundon, West Suffolk 1992

PREFACE

THIS book is about the traditional craft of growing wood by means of coppicing and converting it, in the woodland whilst still green, into artefacts such as hurdles and besoms. In short, woodmanship. It describes all the long-established means of using small round wood, with the exception of chair-bodging, which already has an excellent book to itself by Mike Abbott, clog making and conventional charcoal burning which were exclusively the province of itinerant craftsmen rather than woodmen. The crafts described are not peculiar to England: many of them, with local variations, are practised in both Europe and North America. The basic skills they demand are universal.

Why write yet another book about woodland crafts? Because the 70 years of neglect our native woodlands have suffered, and from which many are now fortunately emerging, have interrupted that unwritten process which passed on the long-established lore of woodmanship. Many woodlands are now managed not by acknowledged craftsmen, but by part-time woodmen – conservationists, green wood craftsmen wanting to practise the old skills, or landowners seeking in some way to utilize a wasted resource – all without the advantage of any proper apprenticeship. It is

for this new breed of woodmen that this book is primarily intended: a source of reference on how to accomplish many of the crafts; and to set a standard for doing them effectively.

It was as a naturalist that I came to the woodlands of eastern England; when I leave it will be more as a woodman. I was fortunate to meet and be trained by a man of Kent who had learned in boyhood the ways of a master hurdlemaker. That was 20 years ago. In that time I have met and learned from many craftsmen, mainly in my native East Anglia, Kent and Dorset. The wisdom on these pages is theirs, not mine, in most cases as practised by their grandfathers before them some 100 years ago when woodland crafts enjoyed their heyday. Any errors in the descriptions, however, are my own.

Although the core of this book describes those tools and methods necessary to make coppice products, remember that this is only one of the three elements essential to support a woodland trade. Without a sound market and good raw material, as history has shown, there will be no trade and often no coppices. How to address these problems is covered in some detail. Modern markets for small round wood are also described, but remember that once you have mastered the basic skills you can invent your own products.

Although this book does not have conservation in its title, it describes what is probably the oldest conservation process known to man. Coppicing not only preserved trees where they grew, it also enhanced the richness of the wildlife on these sites. Many ancient woodlands provide living proof of this diversity, which explains why so many conservationists use coppicing as a vital management tool.

'Learn to walk before you can run, and to crawl before you do either', is the message from every woodman. When you start, try to visit woodlands where people know what they are doing; master the basic skills before moving on to making products; look out for good courses;

then once you have mastered the rudiments, contact a craftsman, who will invariably help to improve your speed and finish, provided you don't waste his time.

I hope that reading this book will encourage you not only to work in our native woodlands but also through proper management to care for them, so this unique renewable resource will be passed on in good heart to those who follow us. A coppiced woodland is the most beautiful and satisfying place to work; a place of exquisite spring flowers, gentle bird song, and cheerful warmth all winter, reflected in the functional beauty of its products.

To those who are just starting, I wish you the joy of it.

GLOSSARY

Woodmanship is a craft rich in its own special words that are still in regular use. These words are used throughout the book, and in italics where they first occur. This glossary contains only those words whose background or meaning may not be fully explained in the text. The names of tools, or the various parts of artefacts, are not included where their meaning is clear as used.

Ancient woodland   a woodland that has existed continuously since at least 1700, and possibly pre-history

Barking   removing bark from a tree, for use in tanning

Binn   East Anglian term for a withe(q.v.)

Birdsmouth   the triangular gap cut at one side of a tree or pole before felling

Black heart   discolouration in the heartwood of a tree, particularly ash; does not always signify rot

Blaze   mark made on a tree by slicing off a small area of bark

Bole   permanent trunk of a pollard or standard tree from ground to crown

Brash, brish or brushwood   the small twiggy branches from coppice poles

Butt   the lowest portion of a stem or pole

Cant   an area of coppice cut or sold in a season

Cleft   a segment of wood split from a round pole (US: split)

Coppice   underwood trees(q.v.) which are cut close to ground level every few years; woodland managed for poles; or the act of cutting down underwood trees

Coppicing cycle   the number of years between subsequent cutting of the coppice

Copse   alternative name for a coppiced woodland

Coup   alternative name for a cant(q.v.)

Crown   the living branches of a tree above the main bole(q.v.) or stem

Draw (to)   to remove selected poles from mature coppice

Draw up   the effect on young rods of planting coppice stools close together – they are 'drawn up' straight with less side branches

Drifts   piles of rods from cut-over coppice laid in rows for working up(q.v.)

Encoppice   to enclose an area of young coppice after cutting to prevent browsing of young shoots

9

Epicormic shoots small shoots that develop on the bole of a tree or pole: they ruin the cleaving properties of the wood

Fawn foot the shaped end of an axe handle (US: doe's or colt's foot)
Feathering rods alternative word for ethers
Fell alternative word for cant(q.v.)
Flake Wiltshire name for a cleft hurdle

Green wood living wood, still retaining its sap, and easy to work with edge tools

Half pointed the bevelling of the edges at the top of a post to run-off water and avoid splitting during driving
Hang up the crown of a pole being felled getting caught in the crown of another, to the extent that it will not fall
Hewing shaping a log with an axe or adze

Kerf the gap left by the saw-blade whilst cutting through a log
Kind applied to coppice, means well grown, smooth, straight grained poles, easy to rive
Knot (to) to remove any knots and branches from a pole or rod using a billhook

Lop and top waste branches from poles and timber trees
Lopping cutting branches off a tree

Maiden a single stemmed tree, never coppiced or pollarded
Mast the seed of beech and oak trees
May-dews damp which affects birch twigs for besoms if they are left out; it promotes fungal attack, and the twigs go rotten in a few months
Moot a large stool(q.v.), usually oak
Mop sticks poles not long enough for rake stails, but long enough for broom handles
Mother tree a mature tree left to produce seed to encourage natural regeneration

Native tree one which reached this country without the help of man
Naturalized trees trees introduced by artificial means, but which now sustain themselves as if native
Natural regeneration the replacement of trees by self-sown seed or suckers, without recourse to planting, laying etc.

Pale a park fence of clefts nailed to horizontal rails
Panel another word for cant(q.v.)
Pile another name for a fence stake
Pleaching notching and 'laying' the stems of an old hedge to induce new growth
Pole a coppice stool shoot of more than 50mm(2in) diameter
Promote to select a coppice pole on a stool and allow it to grow on to produce timber

Ridding rough trimming of rods (i.e. not removing twigs tight against the stem). Particularly used by hurdle makers for rods that have to be kept some time before use: avoids sere(q.v.) spots
Ride unmetalled wide woodland road, ditched on at least one side. Suitable for extraction at most times
Rinding removing bark from poles(q.v.)
Ringe long pile or windrow of sticks, often bundled, and held flat by heavy poles
Road winding unmetalled woodland track, not ditched, suitable for extraction at certain times
Rod small flexible underwood stem of less than 50mm(2in) diameter
Rotation period between successive cuttings of coppice poles
Rubber a sharpening stone
Run out when a split runs from the centre of a pole to the outside, spoiling the cleft(q.v.)

Sapwood The outer layers of a log, which carry the sap in the living tree; generally lighter in colour and less durable than heart wood
Scarf to join the ends of pieces of wood by bevelling so they overlap without increase in thickness
Sere dry, dead wood with no sap – damaging to edge tools

Shingle wooden roofing tile. Typically oak in this country, shingles are cleft radially along the grain, hence they do not warp

Shoulder the end of the sharpening bevel on an edged tool

Shredding pruning side branches from the standing bole of a tree

Shrie to remove the thorns from a bramble stem

Slab off where a coppice pole wrenches away from the stool

Slay piles of brushwood(q.v.) laid in windrows awaiting faggoting

Sned to cut away the side branches from a pole

Soldier stool stool cut very high (c. 900mm/3ft)

Spray finely branched twiggy wood from the top of a coppice pole; used for besoms, pea sticks etc.

Spring the young growth from a stool; so called during its first two years when it is tender and attractive to browsing animals

Stocking the density of trees or stools in a woodland, usually the number per acre

Stool or stole the base of a coppiced tree from which new shoots emerge

Store to leave young trees in coppice uncut to provide future standards

Stub the stump of a tree. Hazel is often called the 'nut stub'

Sucker shoots growing from the roots of an older tree. Elm and aspen form clones of genetically identical trees by this method

Suent west country adjective for soft, gentle, warm, gracious – used by hurdle maker for well grown hazel

Thread (to) to clean a rod of knots smoothly with a billhook

Throw (to) to fell a pole in a pre-determined direction

Thrown of a hurdle, means it is twisted

Trench alternative word for drifts(q.v.)

Turned of an edge tool; usually happens when a cutting edge loses its *temper* or hardness and turns over

Underwood coppiced wood growing under standard or timber trees

Wildwood prehistoric forest, untouched by man

Wind to twist a small rod to form a withe (q.v.) or a twist in a hurdle

Windrow long rows of brushwood left for working up

Wire edge that fine sliver of metal formed along the cutting edge of a tool during grinding; when it is removed, a perfect edge remains

Withe a thin rod of hazel, willow or birch twisted and used to tie faggots, bundles of product etc.

Withy sallow or osier shoots

Work up (to) to trim and sort felled rods or poles

Wreathe (to) to wind a rod

1 *The marvel of coppice regeneration. One year after being cut back to almost ground level, each stool has sprouted a mass of vigorous shoots*

CHAPTER · ONE

WOODMANSHIP

WHEN Neolithic man first fashioned a primitive hurdle with rods cut from the stump of a tree he had previously felled, the craft of woodmanship began. Many centuries later medieval woodmen raised it to a peak of efficiency, managing their woodlands to produce a continuous supply of rods and poles which they converted into fuel, fencing, tools and much else. Their legacy was still evident both to John Evelyn in the seventeenth century, who wrote, 'There is not a more noble and worthy husbandry than this,'* and in the New World where the self-sufficient homesteaders and farmers all practised their woodcraft.

Woodmanship bred woodmen: men whose lives revolved around the endless succession of poles arising every season in their woodlands; men who were the first true conservationists, harvesting those poles, yet preserving their woodlands without planting, and passing on their craft from father to son. This is how they worked.

---

* John Evelyn, *Sylva, or a discourse on forest trees*, (ed. J. Hunter), London, 1786

COPPICED WOODS AND HOW THEY WORK

When the last Ice Age retreated from England some 12,000 years ago, it left a landscape of tundra and moor which was gradually colonized by trees. The first of these were birch, aspen and sallow, strong invaders tolerant of low temperatures and exposed sites. They were followed by hazel and pine, and then as the climate gradually warmed, by oak, alder, lime, elm, ash, beech, hornbeam and maple, spreading slowly northwards and forming a *wildwood* that was a mosaic of these *native* species. The trees that grew in a particular area were determined mainly by its soil, climate and water table. Hardly had the wildwood clothed the land when, in about 4000BC, Neolithic settlers began its destruction in order to cultivate their crops. But some of it they cut to produce small, easy-to-use poles, laying a foundation for the coppices we have today. By the thirteenth century England's landscape was one of isolated woodlands intensely managed, and those *ancient* woodlands we still retain are very precious, their trees a direct link to the lost wildwood, their form the product of ancient management. They are cut regularly and regenerate naturally (fig. 1), distinct from plantations which are usually mono-cultures designed to be harvested like a cereal crop, and then replanted.

Not all trees are native. Sweet chestnut and sycamore, for example, are introduced, and have become *naturalized* in many woodlands, growing quite happily alongside native trees.

COPPICING

Anyone who has felled a Christmas tree knows that the stump they leave will die. But do the same to most native English trees and a number of shoots will arise from either the stump or the roots. Hazel, ash, maple, alder, birch, chestnut, oak and many others *coppice*, producing *spring* which grows to a crop of poles (fig. 2);

their stump then becomes known as a *stool*. Cherry, most elm and aspen produce *sucker* shoots from the roots, each one of which produces an individual tree, whilst the original stump rots away (fig. 3). The trees of America are of much the same genera, and many behave in a similar way.

Trees that coppice can also be *pollarded* (fig. 4). This involves cutting back the trunk at about 2.7m(9ft) above the ground, at which point a handful of poles, rarely straight but suitable for firewood, is produced. The poles grow safely beyond the bite of deer or cattle. Pollards are often found along woodland boundaries.

Stools have the root system to support a mature tree, so that after cutting, all their energy is channelled into producing new shoots,

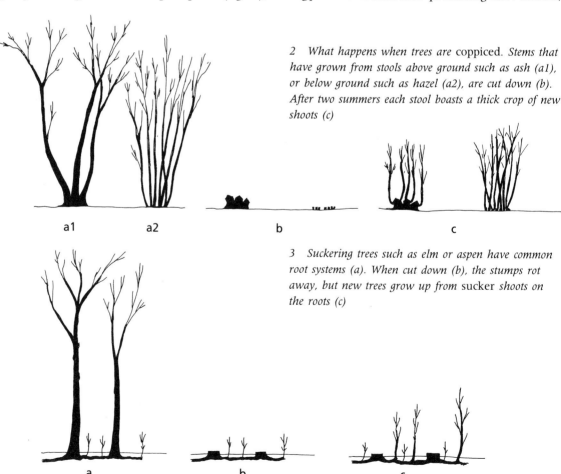

2 What happens when trees are coppiced. *Stems that have grown from stools above ground such as ash (a1), or below ground such as hazel (a2), are cut down (b). After two summers each stool boasts a thick crop of new shoots (c)*

a1   a2   b   c

3 Suckering trees such as elm or aspen have common root systems (a). When cut down (b), the stumps rot away, but new trees grow up from sucker *shoots on the roots (c)*

a   b   c

4   Pollards are cut at 2.4m(8ft) or more above the ground, and regenerate in exactly the same way as coppice stools. They are often found, as illustrated, on the boundary banks of woods

ber, perpetually renewing themselves without recourse to planting, fast growing and free, provided the ideal material for making many products, or providing endless fuel – particularly important during North American winters!

TIMBER

The stuff resulting from coppicing is *wood*. *Timber* is much bigger, the single trunks of large trees 80 or more years old – oak, ash, elm, chestnut and sometimes maple. Although

resulting in remarkable rates of growth: in the first summer hazel spring will grow a good 1.5m(5ft), ash up to 2.1m(7ft), and sallow an astounding 3m(10ft) – as much as 50mm(2in) in one day! If you look at the annual rings of a coppiced pole you will see the great wide gaps of the first few seasons as the shoot became established (fig. 5). Moreover, stools and pollards live for a far longer span than an uncut tree: hazel, maple, lime and chestnut stools several hundred years old are commonplace, whilst Dr. Rackham has described an ash stool in Suffolk, now just a ring of poles over 3m(10ft) in diameter, which must approach 2000 years in age.*

Woodmen were quick to seize upon these benefits. Small poles, easier to work than tim-

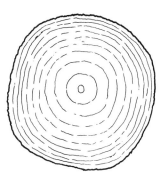

5   Coppice shoots grow very fast immediately after cutting; this can be seen in the wide spacing of the first few annual rings

---

* Oliver Rackham, *Trees and Woodland in the British Land-scape*, Dent, 1983

rarely handled by woodmen in England it was grown in woodlands together with coppice, which is often then called *underwood*.

Timber trees are known as *standards*, growing either from seedlings as single stemmed trees known as *maidens* (fig. 6a) when they are young, or from stools from which all the poles but one have been removed, a process known as *singling* or *promoting* (fig. 6b). Woodmen always had an eye for promising timber trees, and forbore to cut them, although as we shall see in Chapter Three, they did not encourage too many, because their shade suppressed the growth of the more valuable underwood.

Standards branch quite low and have short *boles*, for underwood does not grow high enough to suppress all the side branches (fig. 7). This was fine when houses and ships demanded curved timbers, but it suits less well modern sawmills, which demand the longest possible straight trunk.

In England oak has always been the predominant standard. It was customarily felled in

May when the underwood cutting is complete and the sap rising, because at this time its bark, formerly in great demand for tanning, peels off most easily.

WOOD IN THE COMMUNITY

In this age of oil, plastic, wire, and a countryside devoid of hedges it is sometimes difficult to understand the central role played by wood in the life of every community. Woodland was an important resource from which nothing was wasted. Fuel was the major product: not the great split logs expected as firewood today, but cord upon cord of branchwood, and thousands of scores of faggots used for cooking, baking and heating the home. Early industry was equally dependent on wood and until coal and coke became readily available many trades used coppice poles charred to 'coals', to smelt or otherwise form their products.

Vast amounts of small wood went to make fencing pales, hedging stakes, hurdles and gates: everyone, it seems, had a boundary to define or animals to enclose. Likewise wood provided many with the roof over their heads: not simply the small timber beams that framed the house, but lathes for the walls and ceilings, small wood to make the rafters, clefts for

6 Timber trees are grown amongst the underwood. Recruit replacements by letting maiden *trees grow on (a), or by* singling *good coppice poles (b)*

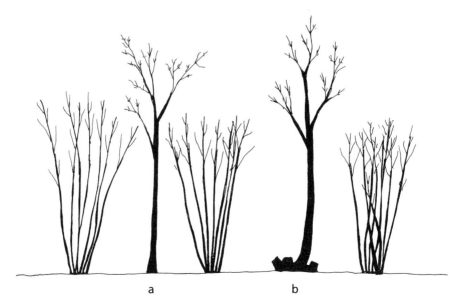

a   b

16

shingles and hazel to hold the thatch.

Coppicing was equally widespread in North America, and although dominated by the need for fuel, the more isolated homesteaders each practised their own crafts. In contrast the English village structure generated craftsmen who specialized in making the rakes, brooms or handles essential to the everyday life of their community. Such was the importance of these products and the supply of fuel that local woodlands were vigorously protected from deer, cattle and the plough.

This century has seen much less use for round wood, its traditional roles either lost altogether or usurped by some alternative. As reliance on wood declined so did the number of woodlands, and many of those we still have in England owe their survival more to their ability to hold pheasants than for their value as a renewable source of wood or energy. That was until the 1970s, when the value of this inheritance was re-discovered on both sides of the Atlantic, initially by ecologists and environmentalists, but then increasingly by a wider spectrum of people who see a role for this type of non-destructive management.

THE HISTORY OF WOODMANSHIP

SOURCES OF INFORMATION

Several sources give fascinating glimpses of how old a craft this is, how it was practised, and how much it has changed over the centuries. (Those who want to delve more deeply should consult the definitive works on ancient woodlands and woodmanship by Dr. Oliver Rackham, to whom this account owes much.*)

Archaeology Students of wood are poorly served by archaeological remains: damp and fungi have rendered most items mere shadows in the soil. Wet, peaty ground however, where air

7 *Structure of a typical mixed woodland: an oak (a) standard grown from the stump of a previous felling. Branching out above the underwood, it suppresses whatever grows in its shade. Different underwood species grow at different rates; sallow (b) and ash (c) grow taller than hazel (d)*

---

* Oliver Rackhman, *Ancient Woodland – its history, vegetation and uses in England*, Arnold, 1980

b   d   a   d   c   d

has been excluded, contains some remarkable artefacts from the earliest woodmen.

Early records Many large medieval houses, both religious and secular, kept records of their estates. These tell the size of woodlands, how often the underwood was cut, what products were produced, how much was sold, and for what price. These dry manuscripts, usually written in Latin, are supplemented by early paintings depicting both tools and products.

Books The first great book on trees and woodlands was written by the scholar John Evelyn in 1664.* Although much of his work is devoted to encouraging the planting and raising of forest trees, Evelyn recorded with great understanding and unfailing accuracy the practices of woodmanship. Unfortunately few have followed in his mould, but early photographs do repay close study for the detail they can reveal.

Verbal tradition Woodmanship as practised in the last century is best gleaned by talking to older woodmen. Invariably their fathers and grandfathers before them were woodmen, passing on by word of mouth their methods, and by inheritance, their tools.

PRE-HISTORIC WOODMANSHIP

Amongst the most impressive finds of recent years have been the trackways constructed around 3900BC across the peaty Somerset levels. Some of these, built of simple wattle hurdles, show a clear understanding of how to use both selected small poles and different species. The wood came not from giant trees in the wildwood but from stools, although whether these were cut systematically we may never be sure.** There is little evidence of riven

wood, but the belief that this resulted from a lack of iron tools may not be true: a stone axe capable of felling a pole can easily be used to start a split, and any woodman worth his salt can complete the riving of it by hand (fig. 78).

Work at Butser Hill in Hampshire has shown how Iron Age farmers built huts of wooden poles, wattle and daub walls and thatch, clearly suggesting the organized management of wood.† The Romans certainly understood the advantages of coppice, their writers recording the rotation at which chestnut should be cut, a wood so useful to them that they introduced it to England. And lastly, finds of Saxon barrels bound with hazel hoops confirm that by AD700 riving and using small wood was as sophisticated as it is today.

THE GOLDEN AGE – THE MIDDLE AGES TO THE INDUSTRIAL REVOLUTION

Although long before 1066 men understood how to coppice trees and produce complex artefacts from them, it was during the next 800 years that woodland management reached an intensity and efficiency never matched before or after (fig. 8).

Every scrap of wood that was felled was utilized: rods for wattles, lathes, thatching, hoops and baskets; poles for pales, stakes, rails, hedging, staves and handles; cord for firewood and charcoal; and faggots for kindling, ovens, drains and cheap firewood. Despite this demand, woodlands were not exploited destructively. Their health was ensured by the medieval woodmen who controlled when underwood was felled, who replaced dead stools by *plashing*, promoted good young trees for timber, and who fenced the coppice regrowth from deer and cattle. As bonfires were uncommon, damage to trees and plants was rare.

Billhooks, axes, side-axes (beautifully shown, in use, on the Bayeaux Tapestry), and morticing knives were all available, and

---

* John Evelyn, *Sylva, or a discourse on forest trees*, 1st ed., London, 1664
** Oliver Rackham, *Ancient Woodland – its history, vegetation and uses in England*, Arnold, 1980

† Peter Reynolds, *Iron-Age Farm*, Colonnade, 1979

8 *A medieval scene: a fell in Bradfield Woods, Suffolk, just after cutting. Records exist to show that this unique site has been managed in this way for at least 800 years*

although some of the patterns have changed with time, they were all supremely effective, for medieval carpentry has yet to be surpassed. And it was now that the rules of good management such as clean, low cuts and avoiding damage to the stools, were understood and recorded (*see* Chapters Three and Six).

DECLINE AND REVIVAL

For seventy years, this century saw an unprecedented decline in woodmanship. With increasing rapidity, the markets for small wood decreased in the face of alternative materials, cheap imports, the mechanization of manual jobs, and changes in farming practices. Coppicing rotations lengthened as less wood was required, the faggoting was burned, dead stools were not replaced, and more timber was grown to the detriment of the underwood. Hard times there had been before, but on this occasion, unforgivably, woodlands were destroyed by grubbing or coniferization, and only a core of coppices whose products still enjoyed some demand continued to be managed with little change.

Then in the 1970s concern about the destruction of our environment became increasingly a public issue which stemmed the destructive thrust of farming and forestry policies. Subsequently attention has focused on the need for sustainable growth, renewable resources and ways of reducing agricultural surpluses. For many of our woodlands this has meant a revival in their management which is now well underway: copses quietly neglected for 50 years or more are now cut over again; some traditional crafts are enjoying strong demands; new uses for uses for underwood are being sought; and traditional workers are being joined by both conservationists and a new band of green woodworkers following the lead of enthusiasts such as Mike Abbott in England and Drew Langsner and Roy Underhill in America (*see* Bibliography).

THE WOODMAN'S LIFE – AND ITS RELEVANCE TODAY

TO BE A WOODMAN

Cutting wood is a winter job, so providing sufficient material to last all year required working all the daylight hours from October to March. Most woodmen rose by moonlight, for to start early at the copse usually meant either a long walk, or at best a bicycle ride. To ease this burden many left their heavier tools secreted under leaves or behind a certain stool, since it is no fun riding a bike whilst carrying a felling axe!

Wages were similar to agricultural rates, with the benefit of fewer hours at weekends and the perk of free wood, but self-employed men could earn considerably more, depending how long and hard they grafted. Except in the largest woodlands where men worked in teams, woodmen enjoyed a solitary existence. But none found it lonely, because working in a woodland is a great joy and never boring: warm in winter, cool in summer, a place of ever changing beauty with each season, and always full of life.

Most woodmen started young, working in the coppice from the age of eight or nine with their father, when they could get away from school. Their training was long and slow, starting with the most basic skills, never being allowed to move on until their father was satisfied. There was only one way to do the job – their father's way (and grandfather's) – with speed as essential as accuracy. Gradually they would be allowed to make a part of the hurdle, besom or whatever, with their father still doing those parts critical to ensuring a saleable quality product, until that marvellous day when the young woodman would make his first complete product, an event which may have taken him six or seven years to reach. Every woodman remembers that day.

ORGANIZATION OF THE WOODLAND TRADES

The most skilled woodmen, particularly hurdle-makers, were self-employed. Each year they purchased standing coppice, cut it, worked it up themselves, and then sold their products either to wood dealers or direct to customers. The remainder were employees either of small factories making wooden products, or of estates that managed their own woodlands. Most products were supplied to local markets, which, with the exception of firewood, were heavily dependent on farming incomes and the weather. Good years meant a strong demand for hurdles, fencing and wooden tools; bad years, a shortage of work and craftsmen undercutting one another's price to get a living.

This lack of organization within the woodland trades was the seed that hastened their demise. As individuals, woodmen could neither control the minimum price of their products, nor stop a flood of imports by moving products around the country to meet local demand when sales suddenly increased. Fitzrandolph and Hay highlighted these problems in 1925 in their *Survey of The Rural Industries of England and Wales*, but failed to break the stubborn independence of centuries, and only thatchers and chestnut fencing makers successfully learned the lesson by forming trade associations which sustained their markets. In America, where specialized craftsmen were fewer, this problem was less severe.

THE RELEVANCE OF WOODMANSHIP TODAY

Working in a woodland today is rather different. The hours are slightly less onerous, four-wheeled drive vehicles make transport easier, whilst items such as hurdles and thatching rods attract premium prices from the new villagers who work in towns. And increased leisure has led many to use their recreation time working to 'conserve' a local woodland. For those new to woodlands, woodmanship has some pointed lessons.

1 Its lore and methods are the product of practical experience, honed by use. Do not re-invent the wheel.

2 Be prepared to serve your apprenticeship. Go slowly. Get each step right before you move on, and seek advice from those who really know.

3 Think like a woodman – long term. A coppice woodland is an infinitely renewable resource if managed properly and with forethought. Treat it accordingly.

4 Any woodman's responsibility is to pass on to future generations woodland in good heart; a steady market coupled with good management are the best guarantees of this.

CHAPTER · TWO

THE RAW MATERIALS

EVERY species growing in the coppice has its individual character. Some properties are shared – for example, you can wind a good withe from hazel, willow, birch or elm – but many are quite singular to a particular species, such as the resilience of ash or the durability of chestnut. Craftsmen match these properties to the specific needs of every product they make, which is why they work so well, and why this wisdom is just as essential today as it was a century or more ago.

HAZEL

Hazel is the finest coppice wood. Its traditional uses have been woven so deeply into the fabric of English rural life, that it has probably had a greater effect on the development of our civilization than any other tree. And it produces delicious nuts.

Hazel is most recognizable in February: the smooth-barked rods end in pale brown felty twigs, which bear the pendulous yellow 'lamb's tail' catkins. The leaves emerge in late April and are broad, toothed and with a distinctive point at the tip (fig. 9).

A HISTORY OF HAZEL

Pollen deposits trapped in peat bogs reveal that hazel colonized the British Isles naturally some 8–10,000 years ago. Its normal habit is that of a small coppice tree, for individual stems rarely live much longer than 60 years, and given

9 Hazel has distinctive catkins borne on a hairy twig, a leaf with a distinct point, and nuts in autumn

sufficient light the stool will throw up new shoots as the older stems die.

Man has used hazel from the dawn of civilization, laying trackways with it in the Somerset levels 4000 years BC. Archeologists have shown how Iron Age men used woven hazel to make their huts, and how Saxon coopers bound their casks with it. The demand for hazel increased rapidly, particularly for fencing and thatching, uses which remain important to this day.

In 1905 there were 500,000 acres of hazel-dominated coppice in Great Britain – some 25 per cent of all woodland. By 1965 only 94,000 acres remained, but thankfully good hazel still grows in southern England where many of its associated crafts survive.

PROPERTIES OF HAZEL WOOD

Hazel grows vigorously from its underground stool, throwing up a dense crop of rods that can grow 1.5m(5ft) in their first year. It grows best spaced no more than 2m(7ft) apart in order to *draw* the rods up straight and prevent too many lateral shoots developing, a density easily maintained by heeling-in seeds or plashing rods (*see* Chapter Three). Hazel wood is at its prime

between seven and twelve years old: the rods are small enough to rive and work easily, and the spray grows flat and fan-shaped making perfect pea sticks. Beyond this age it becomes twisted, knotted and of little value.

Hazel is the best of all woods to work. It cuts easily from the stool with saw or billhook, is kind to handle, and rives superbly either radially or tangentially. And by twisting a rod its fibres can be separated, allowing it to be wound or knotted.

SWEET CHESTNUT

Chestnut is the most durable of any coppice wood – oak included. This, together with the ease with which it cleaves, has made it the supreme material for any sort of fencing, even attracting a British Standard!

Sweet chestnut is most easily recognized from the leaves: six inches long, spear shaped, and with a distinctive saw-toothed edge (fig. 10), they emerge from smooth oval buds borne on stout, brown twigs. The coppice poles are grey, with smooth thin bark.

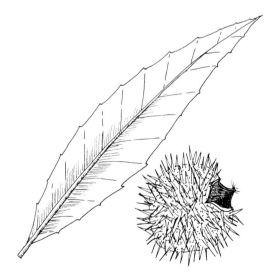

10 *Sweet chestnut has long spear-like leaves that rot very slowly, and produces nuts in a spiky case*

A HISTORY OF CHESTNUT

Sweet chestnut is a native of Italy and the Balkans, not England, and it was the Romans who, intent on a long stay and desiring a flavour of home, introduced it here. The earliest archaeological finds of both nuts and wood are all on Roman sites, although our English climate does not encourage good nut crops. The durability of its wood for any and every sort of fencing was soon recognized, and it has been much planted in both existing woodlands and new coppices. In 1947 there were 49,000 acres of chestnut coppice in England, and by 1983 this had dropped by only 2,000 acres, reflecting the continuing value of chestnut for fencing even after seventeen centuries, although simple spiles are now replaced by pale and wire.

PROPERTIES OF CHESTNUT WOOD

Chestnut stools sprout strongly after cutting, throwing up a handful of poles that can amount to 2,500 per acre on a well stocked site (fig.

Traditional uses for chestnut coppice

Age	Product
12–18 years	hop poles; bean rods; pea sticks; spiles; posts; pale and wire; palings; gate hurdles; lathes; trugs; fruit props; charcoal.

---

11). The optimum spacing between stools is about 2.4m(8ft), which encourages straight clean poles. Like hazel, it grows well from seed, and young shoots can be plashed to fill gaps.

Chestnut has a very high proportion of rot-resistant heartwood, and this together with an absence of *medullary rays* distinguishes it from oak. It rives sweetly both radially and tangen-

11 Chestnut, shown here growing in Essex, is one of the most valuable coppice woods. This stand is ready to be cut

tially enabling small or thin clefts to be made, which because of their high heartwood content, are very durable. Very small wood makes good rods and flower stakes, but only moderate pea sticks. Coppice between 12 and 18 years old produces the most usable wood.

ASH

Ash is the stuff of handles. From axes to rakes, rackets to hockey sticks, it is resilient ash wood that takes the strain without fracturing. This, together with its easy riving, has made ash a prime wood for craftsmen.

In winter the stout grey twigs with coal-black buds bearing possibly a few brown *keys* not yet blown off (fig. 12), are easily recognized. It is regularly the last tree in the wood to leaf. Ash poles have a smooth, thin, grey bark, which is a favourite food of rabbits and deer.

A HISTORY OF ASH

Ash is a native tree, arriving about 8,000 years ago and making up some 12 per cent of the original wild wood. John Evelyn encouraged its planting, a message heeded by many estate owners. But modern forestry has been less kind,

12 *Ash twigs bear coal-black buds, leaves composed of many leaflets and seeds with a wing*

so ash coppice has declined: in 1905 over a million acres of England's woodland were mixed coppice containing ash; today less than two hundred thousand acres remain.

Ever since early man realized that spear shafts and axe handles made from ash did not fracture easily, it has been a valued resource, and as society evolved from using pikes to using tennis rackets its use has been maintained, albeit more as timber than as coppice.

PROPERTIES OF ASH WOOD

Ash *stoles* coppice freely, throwing up five or six poles that can grow 1.8m(6ft) in their first summer. It is best cut low to avoid badly curved butts, although the resilience of the wood is such that poles on hollow soldier stools will not *slab* off in a wind as do other species. Spacing at about 3.4m(11ft) gives the best growth, and since ash seeds germinate prolifically, stocking is never a problem.

Ash wood is creamy-white, with no clear heart wood and very thin bark, making the

---

Traditional uses for ash coppice

Age	Product
7–12 years	rake handles; scythe snaiths; gate hurdles; bean rods; flower stakes; morris staves; truss hoops; wattle rods for houses; barrel hoops; sticks; besom handles; besom bonds; rick pegs.
12–25 years	cleft handles; tent pegs; hop poles; crate heads; turnery; furniture; rake heads and teeth; fence rails; wedges; firewood; charcoal.

entire pole usable – if not attacked by the bark beetles that burrow into felled wood. Older stems quite frequently suffer from *black heart*, often prized by turners. Ash rives as easily as any wood, and can be peeled to make thin bonds. It is not durable in the ground, but is the finest firewood, burning warmly even when green.

OAK

We picture oak as great rugged forest trees, massive beams and men o' war. But this most English tree of all has many properties, so from simple baskets to the manor house, coppice oak provided the raw material.

We have two native species in the British Isles: pedunculate and sessile oak. They are easily distinguishable from leaf and acorn (fig. 13), but not from their wood. Young coppice

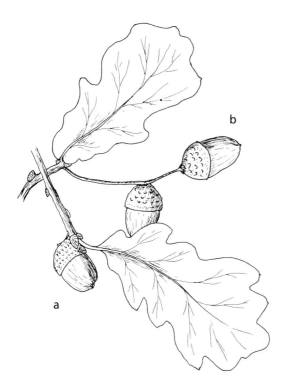

13   Oak: typical leaf shape and acorns of (a) sessile oak; and (b) pedunculate oak

poles have smooth grey bark, but this becomes progressively darker and more furrowed with age.

A HISTORY OF OAK

By 5500BC oak trees were an important part of Britain's wildwood, and today are an essential element in most woodlands. Our hazy picture of that wildwood is brought into sharper focus when a bog oak is discovered. Although blackened after 6000 years immersion, the growth rings tell the story of its life: 300 years old, with long straight trunk from growing in a dense forest.

The oaks we see today reflect our management: in western counties contorted poles grow from stools cut regularly for firewood; on the banks of ancient woods are knobbly pollards cut beyond the bite of cattle; in lowland coppices grow the short-boled heavy branched standards so favoured by boat builders, along with straight poled coppice from large *moots*; but in self-sown woods oaks still grow tall and straight as in the wildwood.

Oak was rarely planted in coppices until this century for sufficient always grew. Mildew and pheasants have been variously blamed for this change, but the truth probably lies more in the abandonment of woodmanship: in coppices no longer cut, the light essential to young oaks is filtered out; no crashing trees disturb the soil to make a seed bed; and no acorns are hidden by man's unknowing heel.

PROPERTIES OF OAK WOOD

Young oak coppices well, the shoots produced in the first summer thinning out to four or five poles. Although older stools are less reliable, many woodland oaks have grown from stumps cut well beyond their hundredth birthday.

The dark brown heartwood is durable out of doors, but young oaks have considerable sapwood, and for this reason stakes should always be riven radially to ensure their measure of heartwood. Straight oak rives cleanly

<table>
<tr><td colspan="2">Traditional uses for oak coppice</td></tr>
</table>

Age	Product
7–12 years	heathers for baskets; flower stakes; sticks.
12–20 years	gate hurdles; hedge stakes; lathes; wedges.
20–30 years	spelk baskets; cleft stakes; bark for tanning; turnery; roof shingles; posts; firewood; charcoal.

whatever its age, with even small rods making good bonds or withes.

Oak bark has always been prized for tanning hides, and special peeling irons are used to remove it. Finally, coppice oak makes excellent charcoal, which product fed the Sussex iron makers for centuries.

14 *Elm leaves are normally asymmetrical at the base*

ELM

Folklore characterizes elms as billowing timber trees whose wood is tough, resistant to the wedge, fit only for coffin boards. But use it young and green and you will find a lovely wood, versatile and easy to work.

Elm is instantly recognized from its leaf – toothed and uniquely asymmetrical at the base (fig. 14). Individual species are notoriously difficult to identify, but an important difference to the woodman is that wych and lineage elms form stools when cut, but English and smooth-leaved elms throw up suckering shoots. The bark on young poles is smooth and grey, but with epicormic lumps.

A HISTORY OF ELM

Elm arrived in England about 7000 years ago, and soon spread extensively. It has never been systematically planted since those trees growing naturally from suckers met the needs of village carpenters, and although coppice workers utilized all they felled, elm wood never attracted specific crafts.

The recent history of elm is dominated by Dutch elm disease (*see* Chapter Three). Although known in the nineteenth Century, the disease became virulent in 1970, killing eleven million elms in eight years and changing the face of many woodlands. Cutting elm coppice on a very short rotation of six or seven years seems to offer some protection.

PROPERTIES OF ELM WOOD

Old stools coppice quite well, throwing up a handful of slow growing poles. Like ash, these

<table>
<tr><td colspan="2">Traditional uses for elm coppice</td></tr>
</table>

Age	Product
7–12 years	tree stakes; hedge stakes; gate hurdles; bean rods; pea sticks; withes.
12–25 years	turnery; cleft stakes; firewood; charcoal.

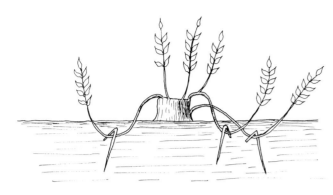

15 Elm is best propagated by layers (after Brown, 1882, see bibliography)

are straighter if the cutting is low, and they are spaced no further than 3.4m(11ft) apart. Suckers grow vigorously, providing good straight stems, and since elm seed is rarely fertile either suckers or layers (fig. 15) are the only means of propagation. It is most usable on a rotation of 20 years or more.

Elm wood, which is a rich brown with a thin layer of yellow sap wood, lasts quite well outside and marvellously under water. Young straight poles cleave well, if sometimes a little stringy, whilst the brash makes lovely flat pea sticks every bit as good as hazel. Young rods wind easily to make bonds, and logs make good firewood after seasoning for several years.

Maple and Sycamore

In October field maple is the most beautiful tree in the coppice as the leaves pale to light gold, frequently suffused with exquisite shades of red. Sycamore, although of the same family, was accurately described by a Victorian forester as '– of a heavy and gloomy aspect, not fit to be introduced'.* Neither provides very fruitful material for the woodman.

---

* James Brown, *The Forester*, Blackwood, 1882

Maple leaves are small, irregularly five-lobed and arise on twigs that radiate from opposite sides of furrowed corky stems (fig. 16a), which texture the poles retain. Everyone knows the winged seeds produced each autumn.

Sycamore has a similarly lobed leaf, but as large as a man's hand. The bark on young poles is smooth, and older trees produce winged seeds similar to maple (fig. 16b).

A HISTORY OF MAPLES

Maple is a native, growing in England on the heavy soils of the south and east, since Neolithic times. It was not of major importance to early man, and our earliest records are from timber sales in the fourteenth century.

It is a hundred years later than this that the first records of sycamore appear, although how it was introduced from the European mainland is not known. Nineteenth century foresters planted sycamore for its dense white wood, but it needed little help, for this aggressive species dominates woodlands at the expense of native trees. Sycamore is now a common tree, whereas maple has declined as our woodlands have disappeared.

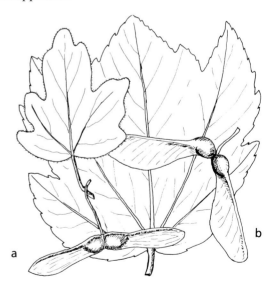

16 Maple has a smaller leaf and straighter winged seeds (a) than sycamore (b)

**Traditional uses for maple and syca-
more coppice**

Age	Product
7–12 years	bean rods; hedge stakes; fence stakes.
12–25 years	turnery; furniture; small carved objects; firewood; charcoal.

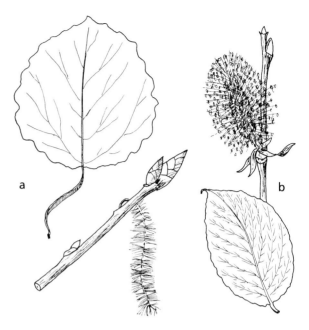

17 *Aspen has a round leaf with flattened stem and large catkins (a); sallow has the well-known 'pussy willow' catkins (b)*

PROPERTIES OF MAPLE WOOD

Both maple and sycamore coppice well, producing fast growing straight poles if given
the husbandry described for ash. Maple can be
grown from seed if required; sycamore you will
not stop. The wood tends to fracture under
tension, and so is rarely represented in the cleft
wood crafts; the spray from both species is useless for pea sticks or faggoting, and poles rot
quickly in contact with the ground.

The beauty of these trees lies in their pure
white wood which works easily with edge tools,
making it ideal for turnery and kitchenware.
Larger stems from twenty year or more old
coppice are best for this.

SALLOW AND ASPEN

Talk to any forester of sallow or aspen and you
will be told they are weeds of no practical value.
But to woodmen sallow was a good standby
for ash or hazel, while aspen made useful ties
for better wood.

Sallow is identifiable in the early spring as
palm or pussy willow when its silky flower
buds burst open (fig. 17b), followed by broad,
curly-edged leaves.

In winter aspen is picked out by its bold,
shiny, pointed buds, and its bark dotted with
the round lumpy bases of discarded shoots. By
summer it is unmistakable, for its nearly round

leaves have long stalks flattened sideways,
allowing them to flutter in the faintest breeze
(fig. 17a).

A HISTORY OF SALLOW AND ASPEN

Both species are true aboriginals to Britain:
along with birch they were the very first trees
after the last ice age. Whilst sallow grows in a
mosaic with other species, aspen relishes poorly
drained areas where it often forms dense clones.

Neither tree produces durable wood, so we
know nothing of their pre-historic use. Aspen
wood has been identified in one timber framed
house, and fifteenth-century sales of *asp* for
millwrighting exist, but Victorian forester James
Brown describes it as 'of third rate importance'.*

* James Brown, *The Forester*, Blackwood, 1882

Traditional uses for sallow coppice

Age	Product
6–12 years	withes; bean rods; rick pegs; thatching wood; gate hurdles; scythe snaiths; clothes pegs; barrel hoops; hedge stakes; ethers; fascines; tool handles; rake handles and heads.
12–25 years	firewood; charcoal.

Traditional uses for aspen coppice

Age	Product
6–12 years	withes; besom handles.
12–25 years	clog soles; firewood.

PROPERTIES OF SALLOW AND ASPEN

You can almost see sallow grow in the summer: 50mm(2in) in a day has been reported, and 2.1m(7ft) in its first year after cutting is common. It is also prolific, sprouting twelve or fifteen straight shoots from each stool, which would be ideally spaced about seven feet apart. At any age, the poles rive as well as hazel, young rods are easily wound to make a bond, and in Europe have been used to make wattle hurdles. Although it does not last in the ground, some woodmen like to make billhook handles of it, saying it absorbs their sweat. Young rods can be layered to make new stools.

Aspen does not coppice but suckers, producing little thickets of straight poles which when young can be wound to make bonds. The wood is very wet, rotting within 12 months in contact with the ground, and should be *blazed* to help it season.

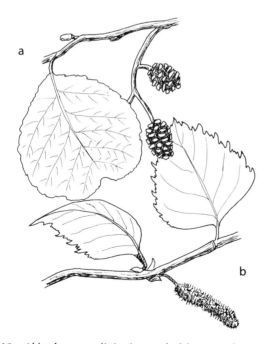

18 *Alder has very distinctive notched leaves and cones (a); birch a triangular leaf and catkins (b)*

BIRCH AND ALDER

English woodmen put birch and alder high among their lists of useful wood: they are the stuff of brooms and simple handles, known in Kent as *dolly* wood. These beautiful trees grow for free from their plentiful seed.

There are two species of birch: silver, with its white papery bark and double-toothed triangular leaves (fig. 18b); and hairy, with brown-grey bark and hairy twigs. There is no difference in the wood between either species.

Alder is quite distinctive – in winter by its stalked buds and brown woody cones of summers gone, and in summer by the deep green leaves that are notched at their tips (fig. 18a).

A HISTORY OF BIRCH AND ALDER

Light abundant seed, fast growth, and tolerance of poor soils make birch the supreme colonizer. It was our first tree after the ice age, and is still ubiquitous today.

Alder likes its feet wet. It is a tree of the valley flushes in our ancient woodlands where it has thriven since pre-history.

Neither tree lives much beyond 80 years without coppicing and early foresters were dis-

Traditional uses for birch coppice

Age	Product
5–10 years	besom heads; swales; horse jumps; faggots; withes.
10–20 years	besom handles; rake handles and heads; broom handles and heads; small turnery (cotton reels); firewood; charcoal.

Traditional uses for alder coppice

Age	Product
12–25 years	faggots; scythe snaiths; broom handles and heads; small turnery; river revetments; river piles; charcoal.
20–40 years	clogs; charcoal.

paraging: Evelyn said 'Birch be of all other the worst of timber',* and James Brown of alder '– we have found posts useless in less than one year'.** So coppicing became the rule, and birch and alder were cut along with the chestnut and other species with which they grew. The cutting of alder for clogs was uncommon in lowland mixed coppices, where woodmen preferred to cut it young to make handles.

PROPERTIES OF BIRCH AND ALDER

Birch stools coppice well and produce a handful of straight poles if not spaced too far apart. Up to seven years the *spray* is perfect for besom brooms, being straight, resilient, tough and easily wrenched from the rod. Small rods wind well to make bonds. Birch wood is soft and does not last out of doors, but if blazed after felling to let them dry, the poles make good handles, broom heads and turnery wood for

bobbins or cotton reels. The small twigs make good faggots or bavins.

Alder is best cut from 12 years when it makes good scythe handles if, like birch, it is blazed, but poles will not last out of doors unless under water. The top makes moderate faggots. At 25 years old, alder is the wood for clogs: soft to carve, taking nails without splitting, and holding its shape when wet. And alder charcoal has always been prized: initially for gunpowder, more recently as an absorbent filter in gas masks.

LIME

Woods of small-leaved lime are beautiful: redolent with nectar, the hum of bees, and fresh green leaves, they are quite unique. And although less common than other coppice, lime found use in growing hops and making rope!

The smooth-barked grey poles bear heart-shaped leaves which are distinct, as are the two-scaled red winter buds (fig. 19a). In summer clusters of flowers hang on a long stalk which bears a long papery bract, unique to the lime family.

A HISTORY OF LIME

The native small-leaved lime or *pry* was the commonest tree in the pre-historic woodland that covered southern England, and although by Roman times it had declined, it remains in some ancient woodlands as the dominant tree over much of the ground.

Traditional uses for lime coppice

Age	Product
10–15 years	pea sticks; bean rods; besom handles; bast.
15–25 years	hop poles; turnery; charcoal; bast.

* John Evelyn, *Sylva, or a discourse on forest trees*, (ed. J. Hunter), London, 1786
** James Brown, *The Forester*, Blackwood, 1882

The written records show little trade for lime as timber, and it was mostly cut as coppice, producing stools of impressive size and age, a longevity which helps to mitigate the difficulty with which it reproduces. Since no trade depends solely on lime wood, this beautiful tree has been frequently supplanted by conifers.

PROPERTIES OF LIME WOOD

Lime stools coppice vigorously, producing a good crop of straight poles if managed like chestnut. The wood is soft, even grained and without distinct heartwood, making it ideal for wood carving and turnery. Smaller poles serve as broom handles, but are useless as stakes. Where good chestnut or ash are not available, the long straight poles are used in hop gardens. It makes only moderate firewood.

Lime's unique property lies in its *bast*, or inner bark (which incidentaly gave rise to the name 'basswood' in America). This is fibrous, and has been used from early times to make a crude string, and in Germany, bast ropes. It is collected by carefully removing the bark in long strips after felling, using a drawknife, after which the bast is separated by a combination of banging, soaking and peeling.

HORNBEAM

In the south of England hornbeam is the tree for firewood, grown as ancient pollards in the great forests or as twisted poles in the coppice.

Superficially similar to beech, the smooth, grey bark of hornbeam has an irregular, fluted surface, the dark green leaves are toothed, and the fruit is borne on a curious wing composed of three fused arms (fig. 19b).

A HISTORY OF HORNBEAM

In England hornbeam is confined to the south east. Although presumed native, it has not been identified before neolithic times, and this may account for its limited distribution since it is not a tree that spreads rapidly.

How hornbeam was managed is poorly recorded, but it was rarely treated as timber because it is difficult to work. It does make excellent firewood and charcoal, however, for which coppicing or pollarding give a regular supply of suitable material, and it seems likely that some hornbeam woods were planted in order to supply London with the fuel it required.

PROPERTIES AND UTILIZATION

Although hornbeam coppices well, bearing several poles on each stool, it does grow slowly,

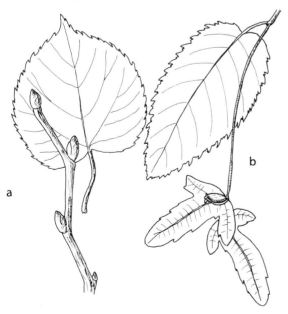

19   The heart-shaped leaf and big buds on a zig-zag twig are those of lime (a); the seeds with papery scales are those of hornbeam (b)

Traditional uses for hornbeam coppice	
Age	*Product*
20–30 years	gear teeth and pulleys; firewood; charcoal.

only 0.9m(3ft) in the first year. This is perhaps because the wood is so dense, amongst the hardest native woods. Since it does not rive easily, rarely grows straight, and lasts poorly out of doors, its uses have been limited.

ROSACEOUS TREES

Trees of the family rosaceae, the cherries, crabs and thorns, are often thinly distributed or solitary, and invariably of great beauty when in flower: a mature crab in full bloom is a sight always remembered.

All have five-petalled flowers with a tuft of yellow stamens at the centre and produce recognizable fruits such as crab apples, sloes and haws. Most have a distinctive feature of leaf, bark or fruit that you will learn to recognise as you meet them: do stop and think before you cut – you may want to save a special tree.

HISTORY

Few solid facts emerge of the early history of these trees until the pips and charcoal found in neolithic sites. Written records describe the value of their fruits for food, but little of the uses for their wood.

Wild cherry has always been valued for the colour and quality of its wood, and with the advent of forestry has been planted for this use. Hawthorns were valuable as hedging, both live and dead, and were used as nurses to more valuable timber species. Woodmen rather used these species opportunistically when they arose.

PROPERTIES AND USES

Bird cherry, hawthorn, rowan and service all coppice reasonably well, forming stools and holding their own with the other species in the coppice. Cherry, crab and pear usually sprout from the stump, but also from their roots, whilst blackthorn suckers, and when left unchecked forms impenetrable thickets.

All these species have dense, fairly heavy, even-grained wood, with a singular resistance to riving. This makes the wood ideal for turnery, gear teeth, mallet heads, and similar jobs, whilst branchwood makes aromatic firewood and good charcoal. Both blackthorn and hawthorn, if you can face the job, make excellent faggots and good hedge stakes.

SMALLER NATIVE TREES AND SHRUBS

When cutting a mixed coppice you will find other small trees and shrubs. Rarely are they of great value, but their traditional uses are part of the pattern of woodmanship.

Spindle Coppices well, and its close-grained pure white wood is used for small turnery and skewers.

Alder buckthorn Has unique orange-red sapwood, and makes the best charcoal for gunpowder.

Dogwood Coppices well, and has a hard wood used for sticks, skewers and withes.

Wayfaring tree Has a soft wood, but the young rods are very pliant, making excellent withes.

Guelder rose Its pale hard wood has found no use with woodmen.

Elder The hard yellowish wood of elder is used for small turnery and skewers.

Holly Grows slowly, even as coppice, its dense white wood prized for turnery, carving and cleaves.

Box Is the densest native wood, making the finest handles and cleaves; get some whenever you can!

CHAPTER · THREE

THE CARE OF THE WOOD

Good wood is the product of good management, whereas wood left to its own devices or poorly managed soon becomes knotty and twisted. K.S. Woods wrote in her book on English rural crafts 'More harm can be done in half-an-hour by an unskilled woodman than can be put right in years',* a sentiment which underlines well the approach any woodland manager must develop: take the long term view, understand that without proper care there will be no high quality wood in the future, making both craftsman's and conservationist's work harder and less profitable.

SILVICULTURE – GROWING GOOD WOOD

By the seventeenth century the rules of good management, as recorded by John Evelyn, were well established. Systematic working, cutting stools low, using good tools kept sharp were all a part of these, but first we shall look in more detail at what they tell us about numbers of trees and how to maintain them.

---

* K.S. Woods, *Rural Crafts of England*, Harrap, 1949

DENSITY OF TREES IN A WOODLAND

Your first rule is 'never thin a coppice': nature abhors a vacuum and will inevitably fill it with bramble! You must have sufficient stools in order to produce good wood. If the *stocking* is too thin the individual stems will not be forced up straight. In the words of an old hurdlemaker, 'If the underwood is cleared of brambles and re-set so as to grow thick enough, it grows *suent* and kind; if not it grows knotty and crotched, and this means more work all round'.* In Chapter Two the ideal spacing for most species was described, and although many woods do not meet these targets, they remain a good guide. If your stocking is reasonably good, keep the coppice cut regularly and it will get better and more vigorous; neglect, particularly in mixed coppice, will progressively kill hazel after 40 years.

Most coppices will contain a number of mature trees, or *standards* (fig. 20). These represent the long term capital of the wood, to be sold at some time for timber (except in nature reserves where a proportion of old trees should be allowed their full span and more). These trees cast a considerable shade, up to 65 square metres(700sq ft), which can slow the vigorous

20. Standard trees left to grow to timber. The spacing shown here, about 12 per acre, is just right; more than this will harm the coppice by shading

growth of coppice shoots that you require, so try not to have more than 30 per hectare (12 per acre), a spacing of about 18m(60ft).

When cutting the coppice you must think of future timber by forbearing to cut good maiden ash, or by allowing a good oak pole from a stump to grow on; this is the legacy you will leave to the woodmen who follow you.

HOW TO REPLACE DEAD TREES

However well managed, some trees will die, succumbing to age, natural catastrophe, or dis-

ease. As a result some estates required woodmen to replace any dead stools they came across. There are several ways to fill any gaps in the underwood.

Natural regeneration Often your easiest option is to leave it to nature. Many trees reproduce quite satisfactorily from seed or suckers, sometimes so well that they produce dense thickets. Vigorous natural regeneration often follows coppicing which provides the light and disturbed ground most species need, and when this coincides with a good seed year, so much the better. But do not expect even the strongest seedling to compete with bramble, blackthorn and dense sedge; follow Evelyn's advice and weed young trees for several years.

Natural regeneration frequently needs a little help. Seedlings often appear not quite where one would wish, in which case use a spade and move them! Oaklings and young hazel are usually rare, for squirrels, mice and pheasants account for many of their large seeds. So do what woodmen did: collect a pocketful of seeds and heel them in as you walk around the wood.

Layering and plashing Layering is a means of producing new trees for transplanting, mainly for species such as elm which rarely produce fertile seed (fig. 15). It is performed on one-year-old green stems which you bend over, twist like a withe to check the flow of sap, and then bury in 100mm(4in) of soil. After one year the new plant can be cut from its parent and re-planted.

Plashing is the more useful technique, much used by woodmen to create new stools, working well with ash, chestnut and hazel (fig. 21). For this you require thin shoots three or four years old. Dig a short trench about 100mm(4in) deep where you require the new stool. Carefully bend the selected shoot over, and at a point close to a fork, remove a strip of wood 75mm(3in) long and one third of the shoot's thickness (fig. 22); peg this into the trench,

cover with earth and cut back the protruding shoots so not more than five or six buds remain. The plashed rod will root vigorously from the cut area, driven by the energy of a stool with little leafage to support and from which, after 12 months, it should be severed (fig. 23). This was a well-tried technique in Evelyn's time, and he suggests the stem could alternatively be wound or slit in order to induce rooting, which if done in June or July will produce an independent plant the following spring. It is more convenient to do it immediately after cutting, in March or April.

Planting Woodmen rarely planted trees. They had no need, for in regularly managed woodlands oaklings grew and odd gaps could be filled by plashing. It is possible that some chestnut and hazel copses result from planned plantings, but re-stocking of coppices by nursery stock is a modern phenomenon. Fifty or more years of

21 Plashing a rod to make a new stool. (a) shows a cut and sharpened peg to hold the stem down. (b) shows the stem plashed: note that a part of the stem is removed to encourage rooting and most of twiggy top removed to stimulate root, not leaf, growth

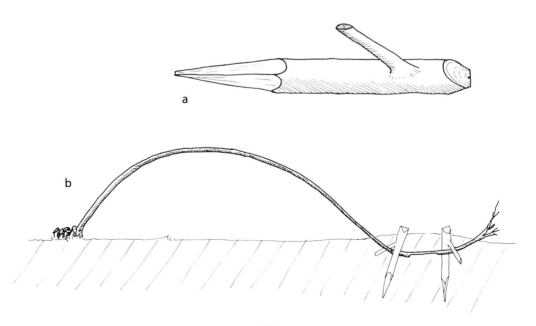

*22   Ways of encouraging a plashed stem to root:
(a) by removing a section; (b) by winding the stem;
and (c) by incising towards the crown*

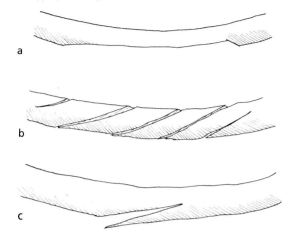

a

b

c

neglect have killed much hazel and prevented oak from seeding, leaving little option but to plant for those who want a fully stocked woodland quickly. Always give natural regeneration a chance before you plant, and then if you do, use local stock.

CONTROLLING PESTS

DEER

There used to be an old saying that 'a tree with a squirrel at its head and a rabbit at its foot is in a bad way'. Today the cry is that a wood harbouring deer is in a bad way. Re-awakened interest in coppicing has come at a time when there are more deer of every species at large in England than ever before, and to whom the tender succulent spring from freshly coppiced stools is manna.

Although more widespread and probably more severe than ever before, the problem is not new, and our medieval ancestors were forced to find a compromise between trees and livestock. Deer, in common with goats and cattle, browse tree shoots, graze the ground vegetation, and in hard weather selectively bark

*23   Plashed stem after 12 months. Roots and shoots
have developed, and can now be separated from parent
stool by cutting the stem*

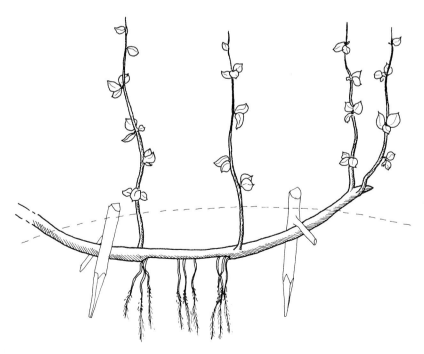

24 (Left) *Damage caused by deer browsing: eating off the leading shoots has caused knotty, twisted growth, whilst one rod has been barked*

elm and ash trees. Woodlands with dense cover, open glades and grassy rides provide almost optimum habitat for roe, fallow and muntjac deer, so they are strongly attracted to well managed coppice! Their continual browsing, recognized by the ragged edge their toothless upper jaw leaves, at best results in crooked rods of little value (fig. 24), and at worst the death of the stool.

Keeping deer at bay has engaged many minds over the centuries. They are sensitive to particular odours and in Victorian times a mixture of cow-dung, soot and water was recommended to be painted on stools as a re-pellent.* Modern ecologists have suggested lion dung, but this precious stuff is rendered useless by a dose of English summer rain. And any-way deer habituate quite quickly to new smells.

Putting brash over the cut stools helps a little, but once the shoots poke through it they are eaten. Cutting as large an area of coppice as possible, preferably contiguous with the previous year's cant, will reduce the damage. But until someone finds a crop which deer prefer, there is nothing better than the medi-

eval solution – fencing. Early documents on woodland management clearly state the need to fence coppice for three to seven years, often by building dead hedges.** To make one of these, drive 2.1m(7ft) stakes into the ground at 1.2m(4ft) intervals. Then take your waste stems, cut as long as possible, and interweave them between the posts, moving the butts along each time to give a sloped appearance, making the whole thing 2.1m(7ft) high if you can (fig. 25). This method is time consuming and can be wasteful of good wood, so an alternative is chestnut paling fencing stapled to posts, which can be moved to another cant in three years' time, and helps another coppice industry!

Deer are now culled in a number of woods, but whether this contains population numbers is arguable, for vacated territories are quickly filled. If you do embark on culling, obtain the services of a professional so that not only is the cull performed safely, but also in a structured way that removes the right number of indi-viduals in each age group. Enjoy the deer, try to live in harmony, but make sure they do not ruin the wood and the crafts that depend upon it.

25 *A dead hedge to protect freshly cut stools from deer. Waste boughs are woven between the posts*

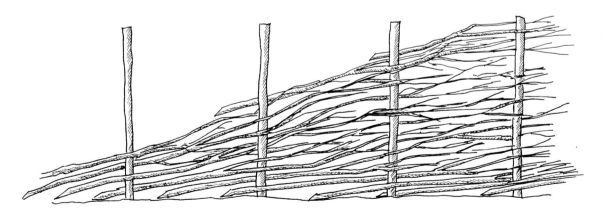

* James Brown, *The Forester*, Blackwood, 1882

** J. Nisbet, English coppices and copsewoods, in *Journals of the Board of Agriculture*, 1902

RABBITS

In years when they are free from myxomatosis rabbits can be a severe problem. Like deer, they relish young coppice shoots before they harden, snipping them off cleanly as would a pair of scissors, and their repeated attacks are just as damaging. Large numbers of rabbits and severe weather can result in stools being barked, but laying ash boughs on the ground provides an effective alternative which they will bark first. But this does not stop them eating spring shoots and you cannot better what woodmen have always done – shoot some for the pot. Rabbits commonly graze the fields outside a wood, and should this activity reach serious proportions you may be legally forced to take action against them.

GREY SQUIRRELS

Grey squirrels are notorious for the damage they cause to beech and sycamore trees by stripping bark from the upper branches. Fortunately beech is rarely a coppice tree, and sycamore is less common in the older English woodlands.

They can be a nuisance to hazel by cracking open the un-ripe nuts, reducing both natural seeding and the woodman's autumn perk. Squirrels are a listed pest species, which means they may be shot.

DISEASE

Every wood supports a range of fungi whose fruiting bodies, such as toadstools and brackets, are familiar. Many fulfil an important role in breaking down the dead wood littering the coppice floor, but a few can weaken, spoil or kill trees. Dutch elm disease is one such. A brown stain reveals the blocked water vessels (fig. 26) which result from infection, whilst in July affected trees have prematurely yellow leaves and curved dead twigs. It seems the best advice is to keep your elms coppiced on a short rotation and at present in no circumstances attempt to grow them as timber.

Many dead trees will have under their bark the black bootlace strands of honey fungus, which produce great clumps of golden-yellow toadstools. Honey fungus is more abundant in

26 *Dutch elm disease: Characteristic dark markings in the annual rings (a), and twisted ends to dying twigs (b), identify the disease*

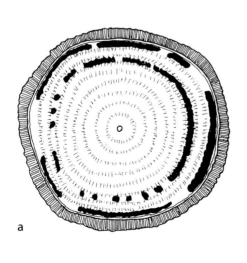

a

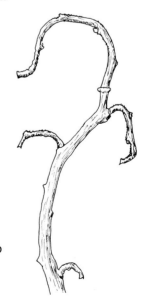

b

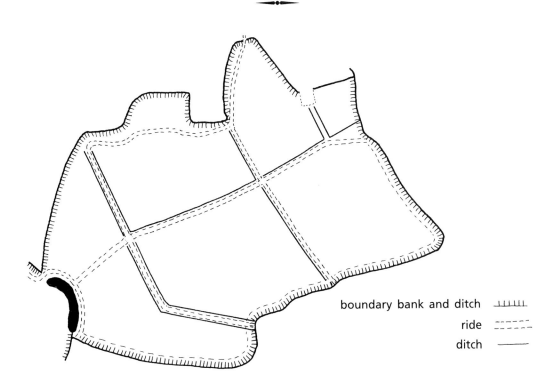

boundary bank and ditch ⊥⊥⊥⊥⊥

ride ⁼⁼⁼⁼⁼

ditch ———

27 Rides and ditches. This plan of Felsham Hall Wood shows: the boundary ditch and bank; the main rides which divide the wood into manageable fells; and where ditches were dug beside these rides in order to make them passable for more of the year

neglected woodlands where it attacks moribund stools, particularly of hazel, hastening their demise, and is lethal to bat willows. You can reduce its damage by limiting the piles of rotting wood which provide it a base.

You will recognize ash canker by a row of often black, rugged lumpy scars running down the stems. It is caused by a bacterium, and although it rarely kills, it ruins the quality of the poles for craft or timber use. Sell any affected poles for firewood.

MAINTAINING THE WOOD

Caring for a woodland goes beyond safeguarding its trees: it encompasses maintaining rides, ditches and even the coppice floor.

RIDES

Rides are intended to get woodmen to work in any part of the copse, but more importantly to extract produce when it is needed. Abused or neglected rides become rutted quagmires which at worst can lock up a winter's work until midsummer.

Rides can be wide and straight, cambered to a ditch at either side, or narrow, ditch-less and winding between large stools. They should be laid out to give access to each of the main fells (fig. 27), minimizing the distance that products have to be carried. Many old woodlands survive on very wet soils and their rides had to be ditched to make them accessible to carts as early as possible in the spring.

You must keep rides in good condition: there is no need to have the 300mm(1ft) ruts that create a nightmare for some owners. When the ground is very soft you simply cannot allow heavy vehicles on it; and if the surface starts to rut, bind it with flat brash (like pea-sticks) or even chestnut paling. Try to do most of your extracting before the winter rains, during heavy frost, or in late spring.

41

Wide rides bounded by low coppice grow a luxurious crop of grass which even deer will not adequately keep in check. It was normal to mow them with scythe and hook in July or August in preparation for the winter's work, the woodman being paid so many pence per chain for doing it. It is easier today to do this with a mower or swipe. Do it before you have vehicles in and flatten the grass. Your target always is to have rides both smooth and clear enough that you may comfortably ride to work in any part of the wood!

DITCHES

Many old woodlands still have a ditch and bank at least around their perimeter. These served as much as boundary markers and a defence against cattle as for drainage, and as such were regularly maintained. When you coppice a cant against the boundary ditch it is good practice not to leave it full of branchwood, and indeed to rake it out.

Those ditches bordering rides were dug specifically to drain them (fig. 28). If they were not kept open and flowing 'the horses could not get into the woods till summer nearly', and markets could be lost. In most woodlands the ditches were cleared of vegetation with a hook and then raked out every summer as the rides were cut. Where they were piped under the rides, these drains were also rodded before any winter rain set in; this remains good practice.

In many woodland nature reserves there may be constraints against clearing out the ditches. If so, remember to restrict heavy vehicles when the rides are soft; ignoring this rule has destroyed beautiful rides for illusory benefits from wetter ditches!

BONFIRES

When wood, particularly in the form of faggots, was a major source of fuel, bonfires in woodlands were infrequent, because literally everything could be sold. However, much of this brash became unsaleable many years ago as fewer faggots and pea-sticks were bought, so that burning is frequently used to get rid of it. Although most hazel cutters profess not to have the time for a fire, at lunchtime in February a small fire is a great joy, and in very frosty weather small rods for bonds or withes

28 Cross section of a ride and ditch. The ditch is kept open to drain surface water, stems adjacent to the ride are cut back to allow sun and air to dry it. Produce is stored convenient to, but not impeding, vehicular access

need to be warmed to render them supple enough to wind. Fires rarely endanger the whole wood, for English coppices are by nature damp and slow to burn. But without care they can do much cumulative damage to both trees and flora, so when you do burn your waste, follow these guidelines.

Site any fire clear of stools and standard trees, for excessive heat will lift the bark on that side nearest the blaze. Thin barked species such as ash are worst affected, and it may be 12 or 18 months before loss of bark and scars reveal the serious damage. For fine, dry kindling to start a fire, look in the crotches of stools, particularly birch; a handful of this with a wigwam of dead sticks over it will soon get a fire going.

Keep your fire small and hot by shaping stuff with your hook to 1.2m(4ft) or less, and keeping it pressed down so the fire does not become hollow. Large fires creep and do more damage to surrounding trees. Woodmen never walked far to a fire, because they did not have the time, so they frequently had three small fires in the course of a day, the second and third being started by moving some sticks and embers on a shovel from their last fire to the site of the next.

This remains a sound system, saving time, reducing localized trampling and compaction, and limiting the thermal effect and size of the fire. The use of fires is usually determined by the owner: conservationists prefer fewer fires and more dead wood; more traditional owners the converse, fearing that sere wood will impair future management.

Potters quite commonly purchase wood ash with which they glaze their wares. To collect saleable ash, shovel the hot embers into a large metal drum which you should lid to prevent rain leaching out the precious phosphate. Finally, sieve and bag the cold ash. If not disturbed, the embers of a fire will remain hot overnight, so that next morning a hole made through them to create a draught together with a handfull of kindling will quickly give a blaze. To minimize damage, try to re-use fire sites in subsequent years, picking them out by the moss and sometimes nettles that have grown on them.

CHAPTER · FOUR

TOOLS OF THE TRADE

THE man of Kent who first introduced me to coppicing uses an 80-year-old billhook bequeathed by earlier generations of woodmen in his family. It still cuts sweetly through any rod, and is comfortable to use all day in a way no modern tool is. That hook epitomizes both the simplicity of the woodman's tools, and the importance of getting the right one for the job. Even then a good tool is only as good as its user, so you must learn how to use tools effectively, and how to care for them.

Those tools unique to particular crafts are discussed in the chapters devoted to those crafts.

Billhooks and axes enjoy a terminology all their own (fig. 29): this is used throughout.

EDGE TOOLS

Edge tools are simply those with a sharpened edge or face. They have a long history, and include all of those most essential to a woodman: you can do without a saw, but not without a billhook.

ABOUT EDGE TOOLS

Although axes pre-date even metal working, heads made of iron were essential to clear the larger forest trees. We have examples of Roman axes similar to the modern wedge axe, whilst the broad axes typical of the medieval period are well illustrated in contemporary prints and the Bayeux tapestry.

Curved edge tools similar to billhooks date from the Iron Age, examples having been unearthed in the southern counties of England from Kent to Somerset. A fine pruning hook is shown on the twelfth century font at Brookland in Kent, whilst medieval illustrations show tools easily recognizable today*, and by 1664 John Evelyn described woodmen as 'always armed with short hand-bills'.**

Before the industrial revolution each woodman obtained his billhook or axe from a local blacksmith, demanding the particular weight and shape required to meet both the needs of his craft and his personal preference. Gradually individual patterns were refined for

---

* Occupation of the month (February) in a *Flemish Book of Hours*, in the Bodleian Library, Oxford, illuminated by Guillebert of Metz, c.1440

** John Evelyn, *Sylva, or a discourse on forest trees*, (ed. J. Hunter), London 1786

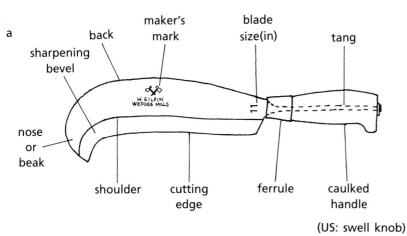

a

sharpening bevel
back
maker's mark
blade size(in)
tang
nose or beak
shoulder
cutting edge
ferrule
caulked handle
(US: swell knob)

29   (a) Billhook and (b) Axe: the names of the various parts; and (opposite) *a selection of billhooks from a nineteenth century catalogue – there were dozens of different patterns and sizes*

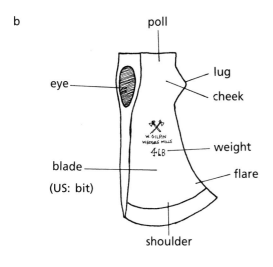

b

poll
eye
lug
cheek
weight
blade
(US: bit)
flare
shoulder

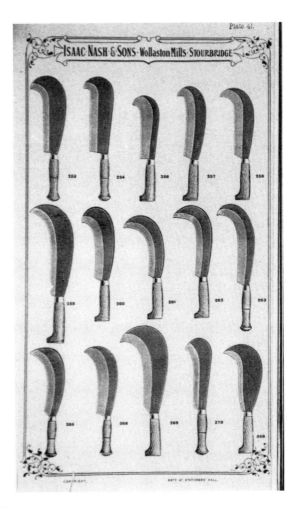

45

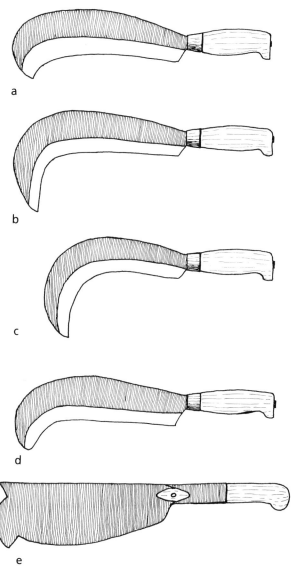

a

b

c

d

e

30   Billhook patterns and their uses:

a   Cutting hook – short, heavy nose; ideal for cutting down hazel rods

b   Hurdling hook – very long nose; ideal for trimming and riving hazel rods

c   Faggoting hook – very long curved nose; designed to trim twiggy material easily

d   Tenterden hook – long nose; probably the best all–round hook, performing most jobs well

e   Suffolk hook – short nose, long blade, one sharpening bevel; powerful, good for hedging and sharpening small rods

a

b

31   Shoulder on edge tools: (a) wrong – too much shoulder too close to the cutting edge; (b) correct – shoulders well back from the cutting edge

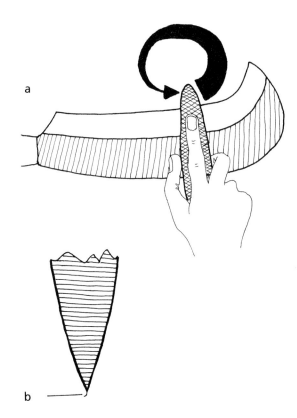

a

b

32   Sharpening edge tools: use the whetstone in a circular motion along both sides (a). The wire edge (b) created when grinding the blade, leaves a perfectly sharp edge when removed

particular trades and localities, and when, during the nineteenth century, larger manufacturing companies took over the work of the local man, they retained these regional patterns.

New versus old Many old blacksmith-made edge tools are almost unusable today. Since hard steel was difficult to obtain, they frequently inserted only a strip of it into a blade of softer metal; after years of sharpening that hard steel wears away, rendering the tool useless. But from 1880 superb steel was cheaply available, and the best tools were frequently marked 'solid steel'.

Until recently billhooks were still hammered from a solid billet, thinning the blade from *tang* to *nose* and from back to cutting edge, giving it the better balance and less shoulder that enables it to cut sweetly through wood. Of late, hooks have been pressed, resulting in an even thickness, poor balance and thick shoulders. Patterns have also been rationalized to allow long productions runs, so very few types are available.

BILLHOOKS

Pattern and performance This is *the* tool of the coppice: you can fell rods, *thread* them, size them, rive them and sharpen them with it. No other tool has this versatility. Pick up a nineteenth century toolmaker's catalogue and you will discover about 100 patterns of billhook (fig. 29). Although bewildering, once you understand how the various features perform different tasks, the significance of having the right pattern will become obvious (*see* fig. 30).

A convex cutting edge, as on a Suffolk hook, is best for cutting large poles, chopping sticks to size and sharpening rods on a block. A concave cutting edge performs best when trimming twiggy stuff, which is gathered by its curve. A short *nose* or *beak* is ideal when cutting downwards close to the ground or felling densely growing rods. But you need a long-nosed hook (*see* fig. 86, page 84) to lever rods apart, or to cut faggots. And a woodman with

a long-nosed hook never picks up a rod by hand. For felling, a hook needs sufficient weight to carry it through the rod, whereas for broche-making you need little weight or depth of blade. Caulked handles in willow, alder or ash, unvarnished, give the best grip.

Shoulders and sharpening A Hampshire hazel cutter once summed it up to me when he said 'Keep them shoulders well back, then it goes through the stick easier; if you gets 'em thick like a chisel, they won't cut'. To cut through a rod the blade must have a minimum of shoulder on its sharpening bevel. The profiles in fig. 31 show what is required. Grind the blade to shape, using a sandstone which rotates in a bath of water to stop the tool heating up, and alternating from one side to the other. Once the profile is correct continue until you can see a *wire edge* (fig. 32) along the cutting edge. You must then remove this using a whetstone or *rubber*. Rotate the well-wetted stone along the sharpening bevel (fig. 32), first on one side and then on the other: when the wire edge has gone you have the perfect cutting edge. Be sparing in your use of the whetstone: every occasion you use it will thicken the shoulders slightly and hasten the time for another ride on the grind-stone.

Once sharpened, treat your hook with care: don't drive it into the ground; don't use it on gritty surfaces; mask it safely in the top of a post; and use it sparingly on sere wood – nothing dulls the edge of a tool like dead wood.

Using the billhook Always use a hook with conviction: match the power of your stroke to the cut required, and never cut towards yourself. When trimming rods keep your hand and forearm ahead of the hook to maintain the power of your cutting, use your other hand to pull the rod backwards, trim towards the crown and keep it at waist height or lower (fig. 33). Sever thicker rods with two cuts, one from each side, or by removing a 'V' of wood and then severing from the other side.

When felling rods with the hook, you should cut upwards with a curving stroke where possible (fig. 34). This avoids cutting into the ground, and leaves an unbroken, smooth face to the stub. Thicker stubs will need a 'V' removed before the final stroke (figs 35 and 36). Many woodmen simply bend the rod slightly and cut straight down, but this always results in higher stubs which are split by the tension in the rod. Slope the cut faces to shed water away from the centre of the stool, and always cut low, because you want the regrowth to be that of a stem, not a branch.

AXES

Patterns and uses Today you will find only American pattern wedge axes available as new, since felling axes have been supplanted by the chainsaw. But occasionally you will need an axe for felling and snedding poles. Axes were made in a variety of county shapes, but rarely to the American double-bit pattern. The 'felling' pattern, with its flared blade, is the best

33 Threading a rod with the billhook: pull the rod back with the left hand and do not let the hook get too far ahead of the elbow. Note also the sorted wood tied with withes and stacked against a tree

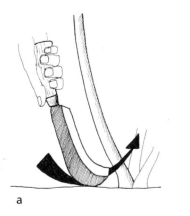

a   b

34 The ideal way to cut rods is to make a swinging cut upwards (a), leaving a curved cut face (b)

35 Felling birch poles for besom handles; these thicker poles need three or four cuts with the hook

48

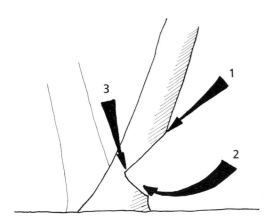

36 *Cutting poles: when felling or sizing thicker stems, sever them with three cuts of the billhook*

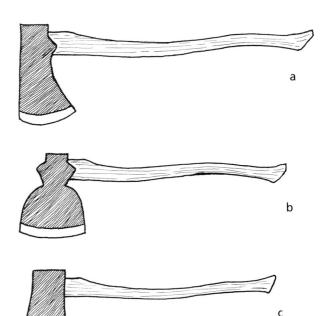

37 *Axe patterns and uses:*
a Felling axe – flared blade, 900mm(36in) handle; suitable for felling older coppice
b Snedding axe – Kent pattern, 760mm(30in) handle; ideal for removing branches from felled poles
c Wedge axe – Yankee pattern, 900mm(36in) handle; the best tool for splitting logs

(fig. 37), because it ensures the centre of the blade strikes the pole when swung normally, and for coppice a weight of 1.8 or 2.3kg(4 or 5lbs) is adequate. Although English axes were originally fitted with straight handles, the American *fawn or colt's foot* handle is much superior, giving better control and a smoother stroke. There are occasional trees more safely dealt with by axe than by chainsaw, so keep one to hand.

For snedding felled poles use a lighter axe or hatchet of about 1.4kg(3lbs) (the smallest poles are best dealt with using your hook), and the Kentish pattern with its broad cutting face works well (fig. 37). Snedding is faster and safer with an axe than with the chainsaw.

Felling and snedding axes, like billhooks, work best without too much shoulder. You should grind and sharpen them in the same way as billhooks (*see* page 45).

For a splitting axe, buy one of any pattern as heavy as you can manage, preferably 3.2kg (7lbs), with heavy shoulders.

Ash and hickory make the best handles, or *helves*, which are usually 0.9m(36in) long, but you can get shorter ones to suit smaller heads. If you have to re-handle an axe, never burn the old one out; ensure the new handle is both seasoned and dry so that it will not shrink; fit handle to head by hitting the foot of the han-

dle (fig. 38); use a hardwood wedge with waterproof glue to tighten it in the eye; and if it ever does come slightly loose, soak it in water, or better still, linseed oil.

Throwing an axe Make sure you are comfortable with the weight of your axe: although the weight does most of the work, you do need strong arms to direct a heavy one accurately. Stand, legs apart, so that your axe head will centre on the pole: too close and you may strike with the handle and break it. Woodmen use the same method to throw an axe with left or right hands. Hold the axe with one hand at the foot and the other under the head; *throw* the head at your target, at the same time sliding your hand down the shaft from head to foot

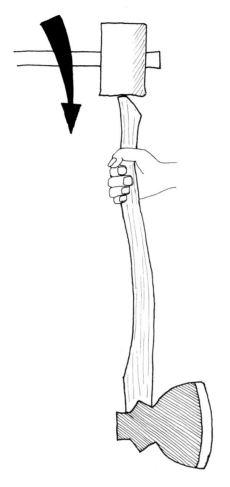

38 *Fitting (or* helving) *an axe head: hit the end of the helve with a wooden mallet as shown, and it will gradually fill the eye*

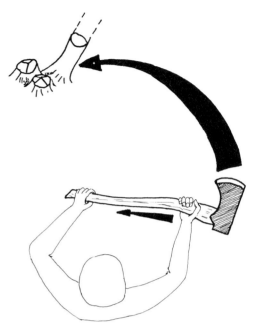

39 Throwing *the axe: after starting the swing, the right hand should move down the handle*

(fig. 39). Your first stroke should be downwards to raise a chip, your second horizontal to sever it (fig. 40). And bend your back to get as low as possible: your hands should be parallel to the ground and almost touching it on both strokes. Aim to leave clean, sloping faces, because shredded stubs will rot more quickly.

When snedding keep the pole between the axe and your feet; cut towards the crown and flush to the pole.

Side-axe or broad-hatchet This irreplaceable tool, no longer manufactured, is for shaping wood:

there are fine examples in the hands of boatbuilders on the Bayeux tapestry. A side-axe has only one sharpening bevel; the other face is completely smooth (fig. 41), making the tool either right or left-handed. The Kentish pattern is best because it can be fitted to suit either left or right-handed uses, and it comes in a range of weights from 0.9kg(2lbs) to 2.3kg(5lbs). It should be fitted with a short handle about 350mm(14in) long.

No other axe performs like a side-axe: its asymmetrical profile enables it to bite into wood when it is cutting with the grain, whereas a normal pattern will pull out. For sharpening stakes, flattening battens, shaping hurdle wood or making your various devices this is the tool you must use.

To sharpen a pole, hold it on a block at an angle so that your axe stroke is vertical. For the greatest accuracy, grasp the handle close to the poll with the forefinger extended over the blade (fig. 42). When sharpening large poles grasp the handle further back to give more

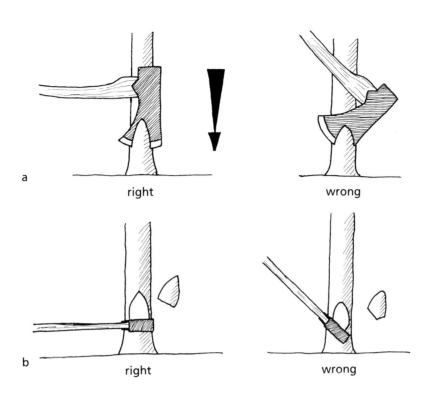

a right wrong

b right wrong

power, and since a longer point is needed, chop several times into the waste wood to help it to peel away more readily (fig. 43). Use the weight of the head to cut down, leaving a straight surface not quite to the centre of the pole.

When sharpening your side-axe never put any bevel on the flat face or you will ruin its performance.

40 (Above) *The strokes of the axe: the first stroke is down (a), keeping the handle parallel to the ground; the second is horizontal, removing a chip, again parallel to the ground (b)*

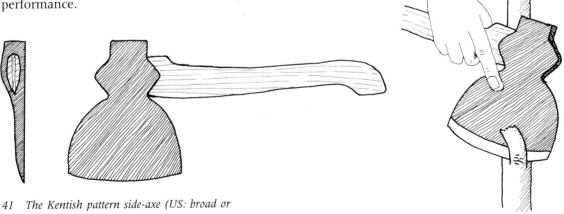

41 *The Kentish pattern side-axe (US: broad or shaping hatchet). It has a perfectly flat face on one side of the head. This one has been helved for right-handed use; reverse the head if you are left-handed*

42 *Using a side-axe: for accurate work hold it close to the head as shown*

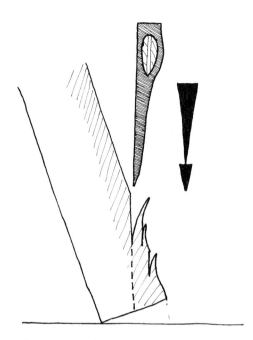

43   *Sharpening with a side-axe: keep your stroke vertical, and make preliminary cuts in the waste wood to help it to peel away*

SHAVES AND KNIVES

Draw-knives and draw-shaves are unique amongst edge tools in cutting towards the user; hence many woodmen wear a leather apron around their midriff when using them! They are essential tools for rinding and shaping small wood, and since they require two hands to use, you will need a device to hold your stuff firmly (*see* Chapter Five).

Draw-knives   These are made in a variety of sizes, but blades about 280mm(11in) are most commonly used (fig. 44a). Victorian catalogues advertised 'gentleman's' patterns at 150mm (6in), it being obvious that gentlemen were not expected to partake of serious work! The tanged handles can be long, or short and egg-shaped, both working equally well. The blade has only one sharpening bevel, which you must be careful to retain, and sharpen in the same way as an axe or billhook.

Although draw-knives are powerful, robust tools, you should remove large knots first with the side-axe. Hold your stuff firmly in a brake or horse, and use long, smooth cutting strokes, pulling the knife towards you (fig. 45). Control the thickness of the shaving you remove by adjusting the angle of the blade slightly; for the finest shavings, or to remove thin bark without its sapwood, you can turn the shave over and use it bevel side down (fig. 44b).

Curved draw-shaves   These are personal tools, rarely found in toolmakers' catalogues, often improvised with the help of a local blacksmith. Curved shaves perform two main functions: firstly to rind thin-barked poles for fencing, hurdles and hop-poles; and secondly to smooth handles for besoms and scythes (fig. 46a+b).

All curved shaves work with their sharpening bevel against the wood, and when working green wood this makes them smoother and easier to control than the draw-knife, which bites into the soft, sappy wood. In order to rind poles a blade of large radius is required, and most woodmen use a modified bagging hook for this. Although at its simplest you can wrap some sacking round each end, it is better to cut it to size, and rivet handles at each end.

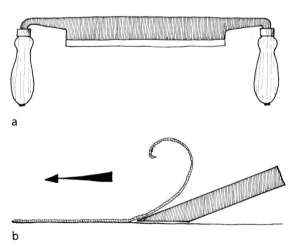

44   *The draw-knife: a typical pattern with long handles (a); and using the tool bevel down to rind thin barked poles (b)*

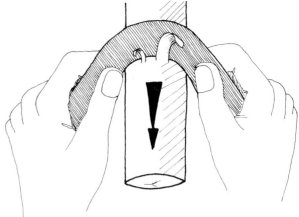

47 *Using a shave: hold the blade as much as the handle, and alter the angle to thicken the shaving*

45 *Using the drawknife to shape a besom handle; note the leather apron, and the curved shave which will be used to smooth the handle*

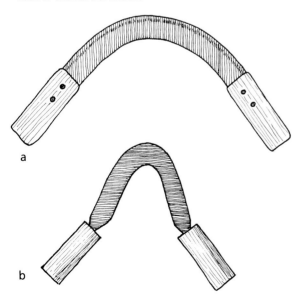

a

b

46 *Shaves: (a) a shave for rinding poles, made from the blade of a bagging hook; and (b) a smaller shave for smoothing handles or staves*

A much smaller radius blade is needed for finishing small diameter handles for besoms, staves etc.

You must remove any knots before using a shave, and bark poles before using the smoothing shave. Hold either tool with your thumbs forward on the blade (fig. 47), and shave towards you, using smooth, quick strokes, making the bark peel off with a satisfying 'hiss'. Adjust the angle of the blade to thicken or thin your shavings, and be careful around knots to shave in a direction which does not lift the wood fibres.

FROE AND ADZE

These, together with the billhook, are the essential tools for riving wood.

Froe Called variously a *thrower*, *riving iron*, or *doll-axe*, in addition to froe, this tool is simply a blade sharpened along its edge with a socket at one end into which a handle is fixed, allowing the blade to be levered to and fro (fig. 48).

Froes come in a variety of blade and handle sizes depending on the job: smallest for lathes; short handle for shingles; and largest for oak pales. The cutting edge does not need to be razor sharp since it is a levering tool, but it should be capable of cutting through knots. The socket should be swayed out at its forward end to allow a wedge to be firmly driven into the handle, which otherwise will tend to pull out of the socket as you lever it.

Drive the froe into the stuff using a *beetle, maul* or *froe club* (fig. 48). An ash butt about 450mm(18in) long and 1.1kg($2\frac{1}{2}$lbs) in weight, shaped to fit your hand, is perfect. It will not last long, the wood flaking away as you use it, but it will never *turn* the back of your froe. Once the froe is in the wood, simply lever the handle to force the clefts apart (*see* Chapter Seven).

Adze As you will see in Chapter Seven, many craftsmen use a small adze to rive their rods (fig. 87). This should be sharpened on its cutting edge like any other edge tool, but there is no need to sharpen either side of the blade, for it is simply to lever the wood apart, not to cut it.

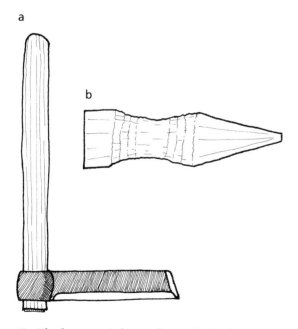

48 *The froe: a typical example (a). The beetle (US: froe club) (b) is shaped from the butt of an ash pole using the side-axe*

OBTAINING YOUR EDGE TOOLS

Good edge tools are rarely made today, so ideally you should seek out old ones. Car boot sales, market stalls and second-hand tool dealers are all likely sources. Look for the good makes such as Gilpin, Elwell, W.S., Whitehouse and Brades; do not be put off by rust unless the pitting is so deep you will never get a cutting edge; be prepared to re-handle a good blade; and if you see a Suffolk bill, make sure it is the correct hand for you.

If you have access to a good grindstone you can modify a modern hook by grinding away the shoulders. Do this carefully and the tool will work well, although still lacking the balance of an original.

It is still possible to have some tools made. It is relatively easy for a good blacksmith to make a froe from a car spring or modify a bagging hook into a shave. But beware. There are very few men who still have the knowledge to hammer a billhook or an axe, and to avoid expensive failures trying this route you must go to the people who know about edge tools, such as Morris of Dunsford (*see* Useful Addresses). Wherever possible supply the toolmaker with a pattern taken from an original tool, because small differences in dimension and weight will make a world of difference to the tool's performance.

Finally, when you have good edge tools honed and with the patina of use, treasure them, for they will be hard to replace.

OTHER TOOLS

Whilst edge tools are the *sine qua non* of the woodland crafts, there are others you will need either to make products, devices, or to manage the wood itself.

SAWS

The chain saw Most coppice today, with the possible exception of hazel, is felled using a

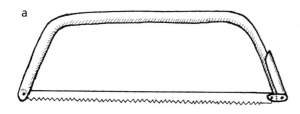

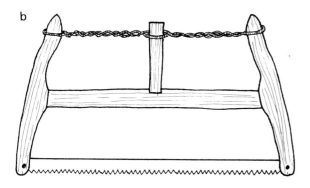

49 Bow saws: the excellent modern metal framed type (a), comes in various sizes; the older wooden framed type or bucksaw (b), is tensioned with a twisted cord

chain saw. It saves much sweat, and is very efficient. It is also noisy and dangerous. If you are to use one to harvest your material, attend a proper course of training, and read the Forestry Commission leaflets or the excellent BTCV book (see Bibliography).

Before passing on, the myth that a chain saw is not as good as an axe for coppicing should be laid: investigations carried out on chestnut coppice during 1969–70 in Kent showed no major differences in the quality and speed of regeneration between either method.

Bow saw or buck saw Small saws have improved immeasurably over the years. Modern metal-framed bow saws (fig. 49) are fitted with superbly sharp blades for cross-cutting poles, which, if used only on green wood, will last two or three seasons. The blades are easily changed, but they cannot be sharpened and re-used. They supersede wooden-framed saws

tensioned by a twisted rope and are more efficient and rugged.

Bow saws come in various lengths from 500mm(20in) to 910mm(36in), and can be used for felling as well as sizing poles. Start with slow steady cuts until you have a decent kerf, or the blade may jump out. When felling, first make a cut on that side to which the pole will fall, so that when it does you do not remove a tongue of bark.

SLEDGES AND BEETLES

To drive posts or wedges you will need heavy hammers. A 1.8kg(4lb) sledge hammer is ideal for driving posts for your devices or forcing steel wedges into large butts.

Steel wedges or an axe are best to start a split but you can use wooden wedges or gluts to continue it (fig. 50b+c). Cut these from oak or ash, shaping them with your side axe, and bevelling the top so it does not flake away.

If you do use wooden wedges you will need a wooden bittle or commander, with a 1.8kg(4lb) head of elm or apple wood (fig. 50a). The rule is: hit wood with wood, and metal with metal.

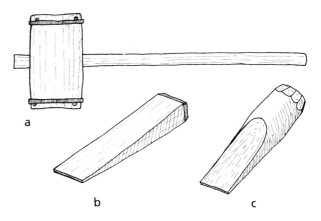

50 Wedge and beetle: the beetle or maul (a) has metal rings to prevent splitting. Wedges can be made by sawing (b), or shaping with an axe, which is often called a glut (c); champfer the tops and leave a blunt edge that will not turn

PROGS

These are poles with forked ends, up to 3m (10ft) in length, used to control the direction of large stems being felled in awkward or dangerous circumstances. They can be used to free hung-up trees, and are particularly useful in handling old coppice.

SPADE

An ordinary garden spade is useful for planting whips, using a 'T' cut in which to insert them (fig. 51), or for making the shallow trenches needed to plash hazel rods.

Woodmen who enjoy the luxury of a shovel use it to move the embers from one fire to start another!

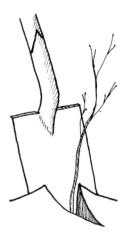

51 Planting with a spade: having cut a 'T', use the blade to open a cavity into which a whip is pushed

HOOKS AND SCYTHES

To get at stools bordering rides, or wood corded a year or more ago, it is often necessary to cut away brambles and other vegetation that has overgrown them. Where swinging a scythe would not be possible, use a *bagging* hook together with a crooked stick to lift floppy stems (fig. 52), or a long-handled slasher. Cut in an arc with the blade low and parallel to the ground.

Cutting grassy rides with the scythe was a traditional summer job for many woodmen, although most now use a mower or a swipe. If you use a scythe keep the heel down, and swing rhythmically from the hips, not taking too large a bite at each stroke.

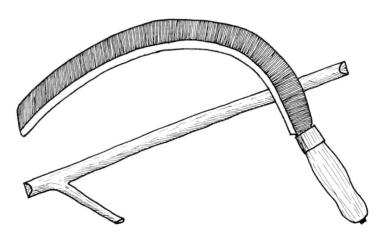

52 Bagging hook: invaluable for cutting back grass and brambles; use the crooked stick to hold vegetation up in order to cut it

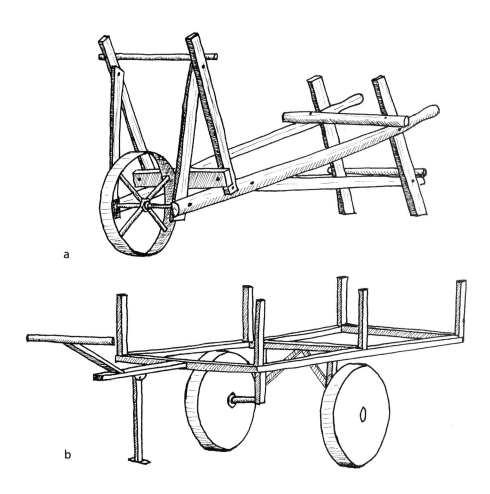

MEASURES

Get yourself a good long tape – say 20m(66ft). With this you can measure the area of each cant, and the volume of cordwood. The rapid measuring of wood when making products is usually accomplished by using pre-marked poles or rods, described in the relevant sections (*see* fig. 143, page 125).

BARROWS

If you fell a large area of coppice you will have to move the poles some distance. Whilst your shoulder is often the most convenient means, barrows or trolleys help (fig. 53). A simple wheelbarrow type designed to accommodate poles sideways, works quite well, as does a two-

53 Transport: (a) a simple but effective wooden barrow to move poles around; (b) a larger trolley for the same purpose – note the high clearance to pass over cut stools

wheeled trolley that one or two people can pull quite easily, and which has a high enough ground clearance to go over stumps. Solid wheels avoid punctures. In a large woodland a pedestrian-operated motorized trolley is a boon, if you can afford it!

CHAPTER · FIVE

Devices

As soon as you have tools, you can fell and prepare small wood for sale. However, to go further and actually make coppice products within the wood, you will need one or more devices.

Known variously as *brakes*, *dogs*, *horses* or *stools*, these oddly named structures will allow you to perform a number of processes on your wood that would not otherwise be possible. Both ingenious and effective, they are simple to make once you understand the principles, demanding only the simplest tools to construct, yet bringing to the coppice many of the advantages of a workshop.

ABOUT HORSES, BRAKES AND DOGS

WHY YOU WILL NEED THEM

Firstly it makes sense to convert your raw material in the woodland. Then you have only to transport the finished product and not all of the waste material incurred in its making. The weight of wood to move will be less, and who would not rather work in the coppice anyway!

Tools such as draw-knives and morticing knives demand both hands in use, so a means of holding the workpiece firm is essential. And without properly designed devices, using tools such as these can be distinctly unsafe. Likewise it is not possible to rive poles using a froe without some system to support and lever them when required.

Finally good devices, well sited, will allow you to work fast and effectively, material always to hand with a minimum of bending and stretching. A good *set-up*, such as that for gate hurdles shown in fig. 54, is an object lesson in method study.

ON SITING AND MAKING DEVICES

Although some horses and stools can be easily moved to follow the raw material, workplaces are often set up to last a whole season. Spend a day or two siting and arranging the working area – this is time well spent, saving much heartache later on. Get to know the coppice:

54 (Right) *A set-up for making gate hurdles. Everything is to hand: wood conveniently stacked; to the right, a brake for riving; in use, a shaving brake; and in the foreground a brake for morticing with a head already in place*

which areas become mires after heavy rain; where there will be summer shade; where there is space to store; and those rides best suited to extracting the finished product. Only then pick your site – one where you can work comfortably with a minimum of carrying, and that downhill if you can so arrange it.

Most devices can be made with the tools you will normally have in the wood: bow-saw, side-axe, sledge hammer, hammer and nails. Some need a brace or long coach-bolts, whilst the large pieces of wood needed for stool seats may require the help of a power-saw. Where only 50–75mm(2–3in) diameter poles are required, use the side-axe to sharpen those to be driven into the ground and also to flatten any where they are to be nailed (fig. 55): this will give a better fit and reduce any tendency for them to twist. Always nail at least 150mm(6in) in from the end of a pole to avoid it splitting out.

Approximate dimensions are given in Appendix Two, but size each device so that it is comfortable to work with, and after making your first one you will find little need for a rule.

To last one year it matters little what wood you use. Hazel and ash are quite satisfactory, but if you want your devices to last several years, make them in sweet chestnut.

DIFFERENT TYPES OF DEVICE

DEVICES FOR SUPPORTING WORK IN PROGRESS

Very simple devices are used just to support material conveniently for use: the frame to hold chestnut palings (fig. 69), and the wattle hurdle maker's *gallows* made of two crotch sticks and a rod (fig. 155), are good examples, and you can design any variation on this theme as you wish.

Sawing horse or sawbuck The six-legged horse shown in fig. 56 is very stable, copes easily with differing diameters, and because the middle legs are much closer to one end, allows short lengths to be cut safely. Put braces on either side and at the bottom of the 'X' but not the top, otherwise small rods cannot be held firmly. For repetitive work like cutting gads you can fit a measuring rod (*see* fig. 108, page 98).

Bundling Bundling up rods and clefts on a damp coppice floor is a mucky, uncomfortable job. It is quicker and easier to support them in two crotch poles (fig. 57). Select crotches that have one arm fairly vertical so that once the butt is sharpened they can be driven into the

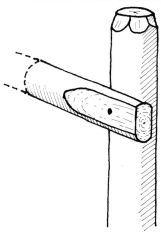

55 Flatten rails on both sides before nailing to give a firmer joint and to prevent rocking

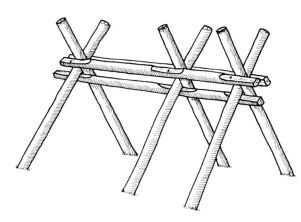

56 Sawing horse or sawbuck: the six legs are sharpened, driven into the ground, and tied by three horizontal bars

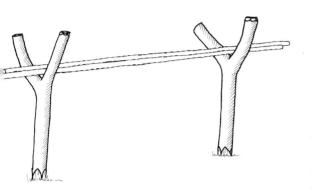

57 (Above) Drive two crotches or progs into the ground to support bundles of rods for tying

ground. This is ideal for bundling up thatching wood, bean rods, stakes and such like, and a notch on the inside of one arm will help you to gauge the number of rods or stakes.

Kentish paling makers use a more sophisticated device. To make a *notch*, as it is called, open the tightly coiled ends of two metal bucket handles and force them into the tops of four stout poles as shown (fig. 58). The notch is stable, perfect for holding palings, and allows the woodman's *grip* to be used to tighten each bundle. The grip itself is made from about 1.6m(5½ft) of rope tied to two short poles. Pass the rope around the bundle, press down on the poles (fig. 58b,c) to tighten the grip, and hold it in place with your knees whilst securing a bond.

58 The Kentish notch, used when bundling palings (a). The hoops are old bucket handles driven into the ends of the posts. Use a woodman's grip to tighten the bundle (b), and if held down by the knees, it leaves the hands free to tie a bond (c)

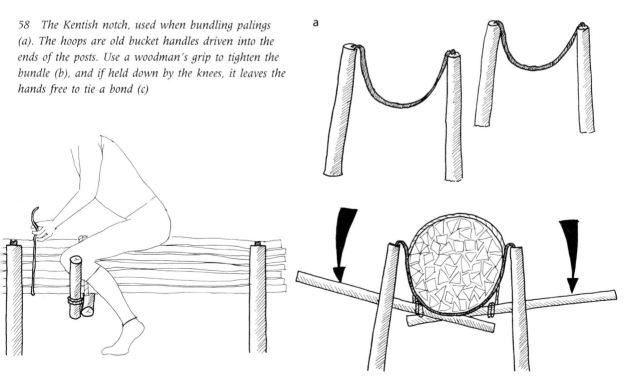

c

b

Rinding In order to support the long straight poles of chestnut or ash that they could be *rinded* or barked for use as hop poles, woodmen used two heavy progs driven into the ground. The very weight of these long poles holds them steady as their bark is removed in great strips.

The shorter, lighter poles more often used in coppice work would slide about if held in this way, so the shaving brake with a back stop and more convenient working position (fig. 59) was devised. It consists of two posts, sized to hold the stuff at about 35 degrees, the longer of which has a crotch whilst the shorter, which is a little above waist height, provides a stop against the pressure of the shave. Brace the posts together as shown to prevent them rocking, and use a gouge to carve a cup in the top of the short post so that the pole cannot roll out sideways. In order to rind the entire length of a pole you will have to turn it round and clean one half at a time. Use this device to rind stuff for fencing and hurdles.

DEVICES FOR GRIPPING

To shape wood with a draw-knife or bore it with a brace requires a device to grip the material being worked securely. There are several effective ways of achieving this.

Knee vices A knee vice consists of a long, flat-surfaced beam pivoted towards its top end, which when pushed by the operator's knee at its bottom end, closes its flat surface on to a bar, thus gripping any workpiece between the two. The cleft or rod is thus held on the flat of the beam, ideally placed for shaving with a draw-knife.

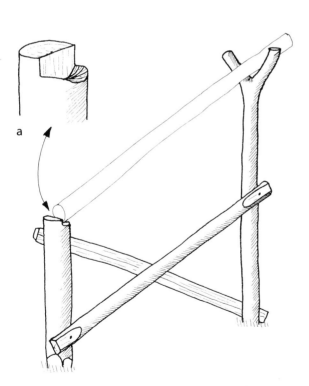

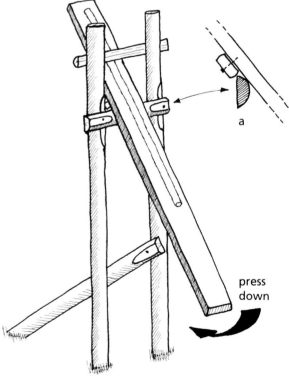

59 *A shaving brake for rinding poles: note the cupped end (a) of the bottom post to prevent the pole rolling out sideways*

60 *Knee vice: a Suffolk shaving horse. Pressing with the knee on the rocking bar closes the vice; note the simple pivot system (a)*

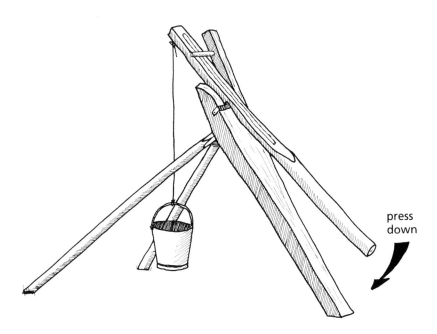

press
down

The Suffolk brake or *ladder* type is the easier to make (fig. 60). Drive two main posts into the ground, and then nail both the pivoting and gripping bars horizontally between them as shown, spacing these to achieve a comfortable working angle for the beam.

A portable Sussex tripod horse takes longer to make, requiring a large baulk of wood that can be shaped to accommodate the beam (see fig. 61), fitted with two legs, and a wooden peg to hold the stuff.

Pivot the beam for either by cutting a groove in the back or by nailing a piece to it so that it will rock on the cross bar (fig. 60a), and if you want to work really quickly, tie a weight to the top end so when the pressure of your knee is released, the vice opens automatically. The very length of the beam, which need only be a cleft or a round pole flattened on one side, means you will not have to push very hard. Use a knee-vice when shaving barrel hoops or shaping wood to make gate hurdles.

Foot vices Many craftsmen use a small sit-on horse with a foot-operated vice. It provides an extra pair of hands whenever you need them, and once you have used one you will wonder

61 Knee vice: a Sussex shaving horse of similar principle to that in fig. 60; the weighted bucket automatically opens the vice when pressure from the knee is released (see also fig. 122)

how you managed without it!

Fig. 62 shows the most common English pattern, but in Europe and America different forms of drawing horse are found*. Make the base by riving and shaping a large butt if you cannot find a sawn beam of a suitable size. Three legs (with one at the front) rather than four, will make your horse stable on any ground. Shape them from round poles tapered towards the top so they will tighten 'into the holes you have made right through the base, and fix them into these holes using a wedge driven centrally into the top of each leg, and aligned at right angles to the grain of the base so as not to split it.

Make the arms of the vice from the mirror

---

* Drew Langsner, *Country Woodcraft*, Rodale Press, 1978 and Roy Underhill, *The Woodwright's Shop*, University of North Carolina Press, 1981

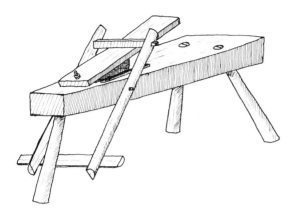

62   Foot operated shaving horse: the vice is closed on the workpiece by pushing forward on the footrests (see fig. 119). The wedge under the work surface is adjustable to accommodate different sized products

clefts of one pole, taking them as close to the ground as possible to maximize the leverage, and pivot them on a long coach bolt passing right through the base. Ensure the foot bar is fitted at the back of these arms, with enough protruding to get your feet on. Make sure the top bar comes down flat on to the working surface to give a good grip; some woodmen add a serrated metal plate to this in order to tighten the grip, but remember this will mark green wood. If you are working on round poles all the time use a forked rest as used by the besomer (fig. 133). You now have the perfect device to allow you to rind and smooth small handles, shape tent pegs and other wood, and to help in the making and tying of besom bonds.

Green wood vice   The two halves of a split greenwood pole exert a strong pressure to close together again, trapping anything that is put between them, and it is upon this principle that this ingenious vice works (fig. 63). To make one, take a 75mm(3in) green ash pole free from major knots and of the length required, sharpen the butt, and drive it into the ground. About 300mm(12in) below the top tightly wind and staple three or four loops of wire to stop the split you must make in it from going too far.

Use a froe to rive the top centrally, and then cut off about 75mm(3in) from one side. Chamfer the inner edge of this shorter limb, and then forcing the split open insert a chip or wedge of wood at the bottom to keep the mouth open by about 25mm(1in).

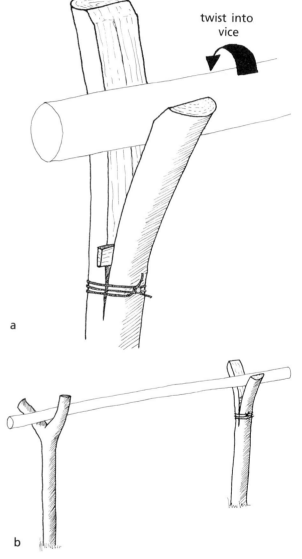

63   Green wood vice: (a) note the longer rear arm; wedge to keep mouth open; and how to roll the workpiece in. (b) shows how to use the vice with a prog to support a pole to be shaved

Your vice is now ready to use. Insert the workpiece by putting it on top of the vice: if it is a round pole, twist it away from you as you push down and it will slip in easily; if a cleft, push backwards on the long member whilst pushing down. Once in place, there is no way the work can be pulled out sideways, although an upward pull will release it easily when finished.

Use this vice when rinding poles or drilling mortice holes for gate hurdles.

Tension grip   Finally, you can hold your workpiece by putting it under tension rather than by gripping it in a vice. The result is a fast and efficient method which can be used for a variety of jobs.

A brake of this type requires two spaced horizontal poles and a post to tension the workpiece (fig. 64). Since this is a riving brake in reverse (see next section), the simple way to make it is to fit a post behind your riving brake! This is elegantly demonstrated in the set-up for making gate hurdles (fig. 65) which includes two tension grips, one for shaving and one for morticing. Judge the height of your post carefully, in order to tension the piece enough so that it is firmly held. And to avoid any chance of a cleft slipping, either fit the top of the post with a 6mm($\frac{1}{4}$in) spike made by cutting off a nail and filing the stub to a point, or quicker and simpler, cut a 'V' out of the top.

In Kent, the horizontal poles are often replaced by a toothed metal *hop dog* (fig. 66). Intended for levering hop poles out of the

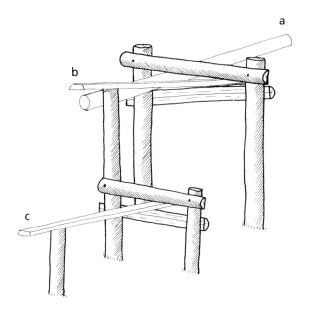

65   *A set-up for making gate hurdles allowing poles to be riven (a), shaved (b), and morticed (c), with a minimum of complicated devices*

ground, its teeth prevent the cleft from slipping loose. If you can get one this is the best method, but you will need to bolt the pole to which it is fixed, because nails will be loosened by the constant twisting pressure.

DEVICES FOR LEVERING

From time to time when you are riving wood, it is necessary to apply tension to one or other of the clefts by means of levering it (*see* Chapter Seven). To do this you need a brake (or frow horse in America), the essence of which is two horizontal poles, the nearest of which is lower than the other, and placed far enough apart to enable leverage to be applied (fig. 67). Their distance apart governs the performance of each brake: they should not be any closer in the horizontal plane than 100mm(4in) or insufficient leverage may be applied; and the distance between them vertically should be about 25mm(1in) at one side, and 150mm(6in) at the other, allowing a wide

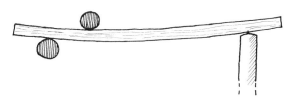

64   *Tension brake: the workpiece is held under tension between two horizontal poles and a vertical post either topped with a sharpened nail, or with a 'V' cut in it*

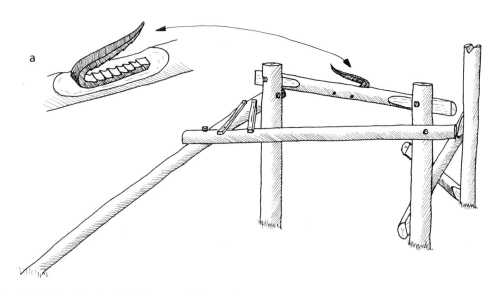

66 *Kentish shaving dog: in this device a toothed metal* hop dog *is used to grip one end of the pole to be shaved, although two horizontal poles are retained to allow riving. Note the two sticks nailed on to hold a beetle*

range of wood sizes to be handled, essential if you are going to rive large chestnut poles into small pales.

The simplest brake of all consists of two large posts driven into the ground, with the horizontal poles nailed to either side (fig. 68a). Triangulated brakes have wider spaced horizontal bars which offer greater leverage and control: they can be based on either three vertical posts (fig. 68b), or two posts and a long brace (fig. 66). You can make either in the space of an hour from poles sharpened and flattened with the side-axe, driven into the ground and finally nailed or bolted together.

You have now seen how to make a range of devices designed to perform a variety of tasks. Depending on which product you are making you will probably need a combination of them, and it seems fitting to end with a set-up for making chestnut palings (fig. 69). It is all here: rinding; riving; holding; sharpening; and bundling – a masterpiece of organization devised before 'work study' was thought of!

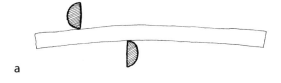

a

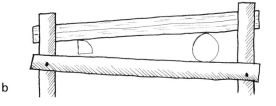

b

67 *Principles of the riving brake: use two spaced horizontal poles to apply tension (a); allow a variable spacing between the horizontals to accommodate differing sizes of workpiece (b)*

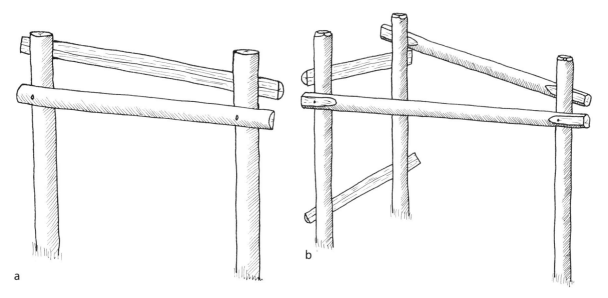

a

b

68　(Above) *Riving brakes: the simplest form is based on two stout posts (a); more effective is the triangulated type (b), or the type illustrated in fig. 66*

69　(Below) *A typical working area in the wood. This craftsman is making chestnut palings; his devices enable him to rind, rive, sharpen and bundle his product (stacked in the background) in relative comfort!*

CHAPTER SIX

BUYING, MEASURING AND CUTTING

W HILST I was learning about hazel coppice, a craftsman told me that each autumn, in the taproom of a local hostelry, he would bid for his wood by the rod; it took me some time to realize that he was referring to the old English measure (160 rods make one acre), and not a hazel stick! Although sales of this sort continue, for the beginner there are easier ways to start than by learning the rituals of wash marks and auctions.

But whether aspiring craftsman or woodland manager, you will need to understand something of the market in underwood, how to assess its value, how much it will produce, and how to manage a wood as an ongoing resource. These aspects all repay care, reflecting in better product, a better return for the owner, and a better future for the wood.

BUYING AND SELLING WOOD

TRADITIONAL SYSTEMS

When coppice wood was indispensible to our rural economy, woodland owners were very careful both to maximize their income and to ensure that it continued. Many estates used their own employees to work their woodlands, producing mainly basic items such as bean rods, pea sticks and stakes.

Important producers of underwood products, such as the well-known rake factory in Suffolk, owned woodlands which were cut over by their own men, who were also sent to cut woodlands on nearby estates when demand was high.

However, most really skilled craftsmen, such as besom and wattle hurdle makers, were self-employed and purchased each year sufficient standing wood to meet their needs. This they obtained at *wood sales* held every autumn. Woodland owners would advertise for auction the *lots* they wished to sell well in advance, and each *coup* or *cant* would be clearly marked in the coppice by means of *wash marks* on certain trees, which gave the lot number and often the area.

Each lot was also delineated by cutting the stools at its boundary, allowing woodmen to inspect its quality before making their bids on sale day. Usually ten per cent of the cost was paid at auction and the balance before the next year's sale.

BUYING AND SELLING UNDERWOOD TODAY

Sources of wood In southern England, where both good wood and skilled men remain, customary wood sales are still held. Each year as summer wanes, notices appear in local papers, journals or by the roadside, announcing the details. These are sales of the high quality wood sought after by craftsmen, and competition is fierce for prime lots since good material is currently in short supply.

Formal sales are for craftsmen, not for beginners. If you are just starting in coppice crafts, one of the large number of woodlands now owned or managed by local conservation bodies such as County Wildlife Trusts, English Nature, Conservation Volunteers or The National Trust (*see* Useful Addresses, page 158), will offer your best chance to sample woodmanship and obtain small quantities of wood with which to work. Most voluntary bodies are keen to welcome new members, and once you have established the quality of your workmanship, many will be prepared to let you cut a larger area and buy the wood at its market value. This is a painless way to start.

You may live in an area in which a 'community woodland' project has been started. If so, it may well be worth seeking permission to cut wood from it.

A majority of small copses remain an integral part of working farms, particularly for their sporting interest. Well-coppiced hazel is ideal for pheasants, so the local FWAG officer may be able to put you in touch with a farmer keen to have his wood cut. And remember you can purchase felled wood from all of these sources, although you will miss much beauty and pleasure not cutting it yourself.

Selling wood Good wood is not difficult to sell. If you have large acreages, then auctions are the best means, perhaps through an agent; smaller blocks of perhaps an acre can be sold to individuals such as thatchers. Advertise what you have for sale in trade journals, or contact local woodmen who may buy the crop and sell it on to craftsmen. If necessary combine with other woodland owners to get a marketable amount. But most of all never waste it nor give it away!

Assessing the quality of wood Whether buyer or seller you must learn to assess the quality of standing wood (figs 70 & 71) – bad wood is wasteful of time and material. Old wood is more knotty and twisted, has more side branches, and its brash is useless for pea sticks or besoms. Obvious winding of the stem, barking by deer or cuts resulting from bad trimming will all make riving or hurdle making difficult, so check for these points as well as for the usable length. And have you got the right species? (*see* Chapter Two.) Finally, be warned, wood always looks better on the stool than it does in the hand.

MEASURING

Metric measures are now the rule, although the acre has not been entirely ousted in legal use by the hectare. For those still attuned to English measures, a full conversion table is given in Appendix Three. Over the years woodmen have developed some very useful rules of thumb, and it is these I want to cover now.

MEASURES OF AREA, VOLUME AND WEIGHT

Area Woodlands and cants are often still measured in acres, 2.47 of which make one metric hectare. An acre comprises 4840 square yards, and is easily measured in the woodland by stepping out 70 good paces, equivalent to 64 metres (70yds), in each direction, which encloses only a fraction more. For half an acre pace 70 × 35, and for a quarter pace 35 × 35.

Right angles When laying out a cant, it is frequently useful to know how to set out a right

70   Prime quality nine year old hazel, ready for cutting to make hurdles or thatching wood

71   Over-aged hazel, about 20 years old, twisted and knotty, only saleable as firewood

angle. Measure in metres or yards by means of a tape, a triangle whose sides are three, four and five respectively. Thus a twelve metre tape with the zero and twelve metre marks touching, and pegs at the three and seven metre marks around which the tape passes, has a right angle at the three metre mark.

The chain   You will often hear woodmen refer to the *chain*, a measure of length 19.8m(22yds) long. Piece-work cutters of underwood were paid by the square chain, but more importantly most men cut a strip of wood half a chain wide. This enabled them to lay their *drifts* of rods with a clear space for working up, and this ten metre strip is still the best width for one man to fell.

Volume and weight   Firewood was usually sold by volume, and it is more recently that customers have got used to paying by the ton. Since you will probably not have a lorry and weighbridge handy, the traditional *cord* is still the best way to assess what you have. A cord of wood measures 2.4m(8ft) long, 1.2m(4ft) high and 1.2m(4ft) deep, totalling 3.6cubic metres (128cu ft), and has done for over 300 years! To make a cord (or wood rick), lay two long poles about 0.9m(3ft) apart as trackway to keep the wood off the coppice floor, and drive vertical posts in at either end 2.4m apart and 1.2m high (fig. 72). Cut your cordwood 1.2m long, and stack it neatly to fill the cord to the required volume.

A cord is reckoned to be half air space, and

72 *A cord for fire or pulp wood. Use bottom rails to prevent damage to the coppice floor, particularly since firewood should be stored for two or three years*

its weight after two or three years seasoning will be about $1\frac{1}{4}$ tons, only two thirds of its green weight. This weight is derived from a rule of thumb that says seasoned hardwoods weigh 19.8kg($43\frac{3}{4}$lbs) per 0.028cu m(1cu ft). Thus you can sell a cord by weight or volume as the customer chooses!

YIELDS

Even before you begin felling trees, you must have an idea of what will result from your labours, either to assess how much you need to sell, or conversely how much to fell in order to meet a certain order. The various figures in Appendix Three, page 155, are a rough guide, but cutting the same wood regularly will lead to increasingly accurate predictions.

Old coppice of 30 years will produce mainly firewood, and anything better resulting from it is a bonus. But coppice that is in rotation needs a closer look. Pace out the gaps between each stool to decide roughly how many there are per acre (*see* Appendix Three). Then either count, or use the examples given, to get an idea how many rods or poles there are per stool, and hence per acre. Finally, use the examples in Appendix Three to give a guide as to the amount of product an acre of particular underwood will produce. It is a miracle of natural productivity that one acre of good hazel coppice can produce 12,000 rods every seven years, or chestnut 2,000 poles every 17 years. Wood as good as this should be cherished!

CUTTING THE COPPICE

CUTTING ROTATION

The age or *rotation* at which coppice poles are felled is influenced by several factors, the principal being the market. If there is no market you simply do not fell the wood. It is this above all else that has led to the neglect of our woodlands in the last half century, and converting living trees into piles of rotting wood serves no one. But if you do have a market, as we saw in Chapter Two each product requires wood of a certain age, and because certain species are best for certain products they tend to traditional rotations. Thus hazel can be used for a wider range of products when young, so it is best cut between seven and twelve years, whereas the optimum for chestnut is 16 years. The rotation for mixed species underwood is usually a compromise: whether to cut young for thatching hazel or older for stakes and tool handles depends on your local market.

If you have a range of ages to select from, always go for the highest that will make your product, because the younger wood will last a year or two without spoiling, and the product may be better: wattles made with 12 year old hazel certainly last longer. In times of very high demand rotations naturally decrease.

Many woodlands today do not offer the choices just described. Many community sites, nature reserves and old farm copses may either be neglected or may be cut to meet objectives of greater importance than solely the best use of the wood. In this position simply turn the traditional process on its head and develop the best markets for that material which is available (*see* Chapter Fourteen).

PLANNING A CUT

When to cut Follow the acknowledged wisdom of cutting only when the leaf is off and the sap down. There are good reasons for this: being moister, sappy wood loses its bark more quickly and lasts less time in the ground; whilst shoots sprouted in middle or late summer have little time to harden off before winter and can be less frost-hardy. Hazel cutters start when the nut is loose in the husk, which is September, but cutting normally begins in October or November, and should always finish by Lady Day, March 25th, times already well established when Evelyn set them down 300 years ago.

In woodland nature reserves, cutting may have to finish earlier in order to avoid damaging sensitive plants.

How much to cut Most beginners are over-optimistic about what they can achieve! Get an idea of what you can handle before committing yourself to a large area, and remember an experienced hazel cutter working full time will take a week to fell one acre, and up to five weeks working this up, depending which products he makes.

73 *Cutting plan for a part of a wood, showing the rides and fells or cants. Each is dated to show when it was cut (an eight year cycle) whilst the dashed lines show how each cant is best cut in strips to give easy access to the rides*

Once established, with firm orders and knowing the wood you are felling, you can estimate what size cant you require. But never cut less than half an acre: small areas with a high proportion of 'edge', suffer excessive shade and greater deer damage, both of which will spoil regeneration. You can fell more if you work-up less material during the winter. Hazel craftsmen often felled sufficient to give them work throughout the summer, making wattle hurdles and faggots until the end of June, spars and broches in July, hay cribs during July and August, and finishing August by scything the rides prior to the next seasons cut. Consider spending March just felling and bundling for later use.

Access, timber and fencing There are one or two other points still to consider before putting billhook to wood, and failure to do so always results in extra work!

Firstly make sure you know where to store the poles you are about to fell, and that the area is adjacent to a ride so they can be easily extracted (fig. 73). Ensure your planned work will not deny access to other areas, resulting in the damaging task of extracting through growing coppice. And where possible aim to extract your produce downhill.

I explained in earlier chapters how most

74 Keep records to show how the wood is cut and what it produces. This information is as vital to historians and ecologists as to the woodland manager

coppices contain timber trees. Occasionally some of these will be felled, a task normally performed at the end of the season. If this is the case, make sure your plans accommodate it by not placing cords where these standards will be thrown. Another necessary consideration is fencing the finished cant against deer (*see* Chapter Three). Build into your plan how and when you will accomplish this.

Records Keep a detailed log of everything you do (fig. 74). A map is an essential aid to this. Record the date, which area was cut, what it produced, any planting, fencing or maintenance undertaken, and any comments on the quality of the wood that will help you with your planning in the future. It is usual to signify each felling by the year in which it finished, i.e.: a cant completed in March 1992 is called 'the '92 cant'.

If you are working in one wood continuously, your records will not only help you to know your wood better, but will provide a vital historical record to those that follow, so that they may understand and interpret what you have done.

METHODS OF CUTTING COPPICE

At last! Having planned what, where, when and how much to cut, you may start. During your cutting maintain that same sense of order you have built into your plan: work safely, know where everything has to go, and only do a job once.

Date	Fell	Age	Area cut	Produced
91/92	South	17 yrs	1 acre (see map)	3 cords 70 bundles thatching rods 800 hedging stakes 200 tree stakes 40 bundles pea sticks

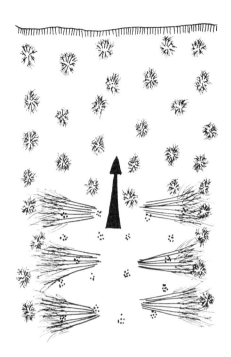

a

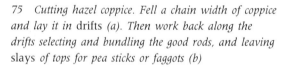

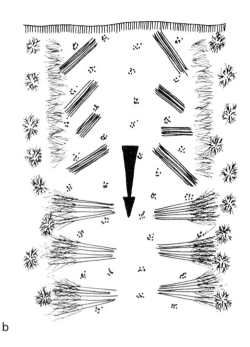

b

75 Cutting hazel coppice. Fell a chain width of coppice and lay it in drifts (a). Then work back along the drifts selecting and bundling the good rods, and leaving slays of tops for pea sticks or faggots (b)

Cutting hazel coppice If you are working alone cut a strip 10m(11yds) wide, starting at one side and working across. Lay the cut stems in two *drifts* or *streams*, at either side of the strip, butt ends to the centre and with a good working gap between them (fig. 75). Keep the butts together and level, but fan out the tops, which will make them easier to separate later. Always start from the ride, and it you can, cut up-hill. Cut right through to the boundary of your cant, then turn around and come back through what you have felled, working it up. Once again, work to a logical pattern: throw pea sticks and faggoting to one side in a long *slay* to be bundled up as the last job of all; throw good rods to the other in separate groups for thatching, hurdle making, shores, and lastly fine rods for withes. Bundle these as you go.

Once this is complete, start another 10 metre strip. If you are to make hurdles, carry on until you have completed about one acre before setting up your pitch; more than this will give you too much carrying. The advantage of these narrow strips is that should the weather or other problems foreshorten your planned cut, you always have a line at which you can finish without trapping uncut coppice behind that which you have already cut.

Cutting mixed or chestnut coppice These poles are cut at a much larger size than hazel, often being twice the age, and demanding a different approach. Start at the ride as for hazel, and cut the same width (or double if two of you are working together), but work up the felled poles as you go. To one side leave a slay of tops for pea sticks and faggoting, to the other poles sorted for various uses – tool handles, gate hurdle wood, thatching wood and cord. Take these to the ride frequently to keep the floor clean (fig. 76). Normally the useless brash is burned whilst working, since not all species produce spray that is of any use, a problem

today when virtually no-one uses faggots for firing.

The proper cutting of stools   As with every aspect of coppice work, there is a right and a wrong way of cutting. Established methods evolved to safeguard both the future of the wood and its quality. The advice given by John Evelyn is still pertinent today: 'The cutting slanting smooth and close is of great importance. . . . Cut not above half a foot from the ground, nay the closer the better'.* The benefits of cutting low

76   *A cant in March, with all the stools cut low, all top and cord wood cleared away. The marked standard trees have been left for timber, but one has been felled. Young coppice is growing in the background*

were described by James Brown: 'shoots . . . which proceed from that part of the stock which rises two inches above the ground, . . . will partake more of the character of branches than of trees . . . '.** So to grow straight poles, you must cut low (fig. 77).

Slope your cuts away from the centre of

---

* John Evelyn, *Sylva, or a discourse on forest trees*, (ed. J. Hunter), London, 1786

** James Brown, *The Forester*, Blackwood, 1882

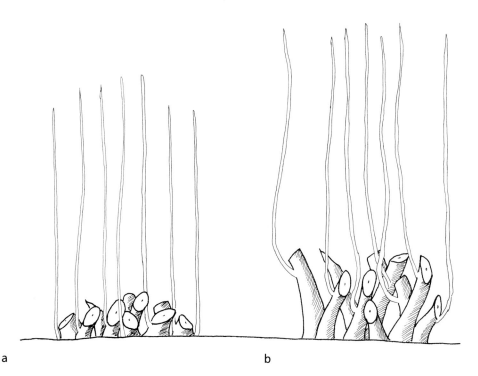

a   b

the stool so that water is not shed into its heart causing it to rot. Smooth cut surfaces serve the same purpose by not offering jagged edges in which water will lodge; use the methods described in Chapter Four to avoid this problem. More importantly when cutting stools, avoid lifting or peeling away the bark, for this not only provides a perfect place for decay to start, but loose bark results in fewer new shoots the following spring. The more quickly stools rot, the fewer you will have the next time, causing more work to replace them. As we have seen, cutting upwards rather than downwards where possible reduces this problem. Always bear in mind your obligation to woodmen yet to come.

77 Coppice stems should be cut low, as in (a), causing new rods to spring from the stool; in (b) stems were cut too high, resulting in the new rods being curved as they spring from stubs rather than stools

CHAPTER · SEVEN

RIVING WOOD

WHEN a local woodman came in search of wood to buy from the coppice in which I work, one of his first actions was to cut a two foot rod of hazel and rive it perfectly into two pieces using his billhook – 'to see what it's like'. It was an action performed with deceptive ease, frustratingly difficult to emulate. The ability to rive wood of any size properly is essential to most of the coppice crafts. This chapter will give you an understanding of how this outwardly simple process works. But only through practice will you experience what words are inadequate to portray: the feel and sound of wood cleaving straight and true in your hands.

You will find the word *cleft* used many times in this chapter. The dictionary defines a cleft as a split or crack; to most woodmen it is the piece of wood resulting from the process of cleaving or riving, and it is in this sense that I use the word.

ABOUT RIVEN WOOD

THE HISTORICAL RECORD

How early man, struggling to survive in the wildwood, first came to rive wood must remain a conjecture. Whether he saw a damaged tree split down its stem, or whether a pole split up from the base while being wrenched or cut from a stool, he must have quickly realised the value of cleft rods and poles for many of his everyday needs. The oldest examples are the coppice wood hurdles that have been preserved for 6,000 years in the peat of the Somerset Levels. Iron-age huts used hazel clefts which, daubed with mud, provided substantial walls, and by the first century AD riven oak shingles for roofing hovels were being made in the southern counties of England.

As the Somerset discoveries show, this skill pre-dates metal tools. Wood is riven not by cutting but by levering it apart, and once the process is started in a small rod it can be continued and controlled without tools (fig. 78). A flint with a sharpened edge can start a split in a green hazel rod as well as a billhook, so small cleft wood has been a valuable resource since probably the Neolithic period. As both steel tools and the craftsman's skill developed, the thin rods in those Iron Age walls were replaced by the 6mm($\frac{1}{4}$in) thick lathes used in the walls and ceilings of millions of houses until well into this century. Even today thatch is fixed by

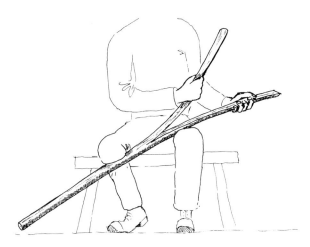

78 Riving by hand, levering the pole against the legs to control the direction of the split

fine clefts of hazel known as broches. Fencing has always been the biggest user of cleft wood, whether as posts and pales for deer parks and gardens, as gate or wattle hurdles used by sheep farmers, or as the chestnut pale and wire fencing familiar today. When slack barrels and crates were the main means of transporting the output of England's growing industry, it was cleft hoops and rods that went into the making of them, whilst even today wooden tent pegs are shaped only from clefts.

WHY RIVE WOOD?

A process as old as woodmanship itself, and fundamental to so many crafts, must have much to commend it. Riving does: it is fast, ideal for small wood, and the resultant clefts have advantages in strength and longevity unobtainable by any other process.

Small wood is the raw material for coppice products, it being uncommon to use poles of more than 15 summers' growth. However well stocked the coppice and however kind the growth, few poles are ever truly straight, so that trying to saw along their length is wasteful and requires quite large wood. Riving on the other hand allows the craftsman to cut his

wood much smaller and younger, and his ingenuity has developed subtle methods to incorporate wavy, *wound* and even forked material into saleable, durable products. Another benefit is that the edge tools used such as billhook and froe create no kerf and hence no wasteful sawdust. Also speed is essential to achieve competitive costs, and riving is much faster than sawing.

In regular use, products such as hurdles, wattles and fencing suffer a hard life – they are thumped and humped by man or beast, and exposed to rain, frost and sun. Durability and strength are thus important assets, and cleft wood has both in greater measure, size for size, than sawn wood. When a pole is riven, the wood fibres are parted from one another along their length. A few are torn, and raised as spears, but the face of a cleft presents a ribbed-rough surface of remarkable continuity, following every curve and fold of the pole's growth, even around knots. Because the wood vessels have not been cut across, exposing their open ends, this surface is uniquely waterproof, and explains why cleft pales in oak or chestnut have stood in damp shade on park banks for over three-quarters of a century. Further, since they follow the natural flow of the grain rather than cutting across it as do sawn lengths, there are fewer points of weakness that might fracture under stress, and indeed the very process of riving frequently reveals weaknesses that sawing would not. This virtue was appreciated beyond the coppice, particularly where reliable strength was essential: Welsh miners insisted that all their hewing-axe handles should be fashioned from cleft ash, and wheelwrights did likewise for their spokes.

THE ART OF RIVING WOOD

THE BASIC PRINCIPLES OF RIVING

Always start riving at the smaller end of a pole, thereby ensuring that any *running-out* of the split occurs towards the thicker end. This gives a much better chance of having two usable clefts, albeit one a little thicker than the other. Where possible it is better to rive wood into two equal segments: riving unequal clefts, although inevitable with certain sizes of wood, demands considerably more care since the thinner cleft flexes more than the thicker, and hence tends to run-out. Where branches occur on opposite sides of a rod, such as hazel, you should always split between the knots, not through them (fig. 79).

A split is started by driving a froe, adze or billhook into the end of the piece and is continued by levering the two clefts apart, normally still using the splitting tool, although a skilled man can rive a pole by literally pulling it apart (fig. 78).

This ancient method demonstrates the essence of riving: that with even pressure on

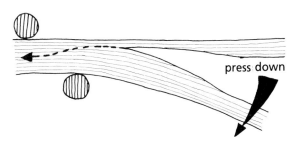

80   *Correcting a split which has run out: apply tension to the thicker cleft and the split will return as shown*

both clefts a split runs true, but varying pressure will always cause it to run towards the cleft under greater tension. This knowledge allows you to correct a run-out split by applying tension to the thicker cleft (fig. 80), a job made easier by the use of a *riving brake*, in which the necessary pressure can be applied in a controlled and effective manner.

You should not cut along the grain unless you need to chop though a large knot. That a rod is being riven centrally requires little or no close inspection once you have mastered the craft: the clefts separate with a crisp, clear, unmistakable cra-a-ck; whilst your hands sense the similar resistance of even clefts, and the sharp separation of cleanly riven surfaces. This 'feel' allows a skilled man to rive almost without looking, and to work at remarkable speed: a good day's work for a thatching spar maker is 1600 spars.

SELECTING THE RIGHT QUALITY WOOD

Not all wood rives well. In addition to the differences between species which were discussed in Chapter Two, are those resulting from the site, the genetic make-up of the tree, and even the way it has been managed. Wood from hedgerows or exposed sites at the edge of a coppice rarely makes good product, its grain *winding* as a result of the constant rotating movement of the crown to wind and sun. Suffolk woodmen often speak of *red* ash, which apart from a blush of colour described by the

79   *Riving rods: where possible your split should pass between the knots, not through them*

name, possesses a stringy grain resistant to riving and is locally prized for making rake heads since it does not split when the teeth are driven in. It occurs randomly amongst the ash stools of their local woods.

Ash, hazel, willow and sweet chestnut all rive superbly in a variety of sizes, and are the backbone of the cleft-wood trades. Oak and elm also rive well when grown fast and clean, but most other coppice woods do not, or like alder and birch rot so quickly as to make them useless.

However, even the best material from a favoured site may be of no use if it is not in the right condition. Wood for riving must have the right degree of moisture, *greenness* and toughness. After January, when the sap has started rising, hazel rods are too green when cut to be made into broches immediately, for the split frequently runs out, and they should be stored for four to six weeks before riving. Similarly, ash poles for gate hurdles are best stored until the summer to 'toughen up'. Willow and chestnut, however, can be used from the stool. Conversely *sere* wood, having lost its resilience, is useless, continually breaking when put under tension.

To provide winter-felled wood for working up in the summer, you must practise the woodman's knack for keeping wood in good condition. If you want to save hazel rods for wattle hurdles or broches, *ridd* them – leave about 25mm(1in) of the small twigs on – because if you knot them flush and remove any bark, that area will dry in early summer and then break when riven or wound. And store

all your poles or rods out of the direct sunlight which will dry them too fast, but away from damp which will encourage fungal attack and ruin them. Standing the bundles on end under a large tree works well – it is shady and allows a good air flow.

DIFFERENT METHODS OF RIVING

USING WEDGES ON LARGE POLES

Poles much greater in diameter than 150mm (6in) are difficult to rive with a froe in a brake: the wooden beetle is barely heavy enough to drive a froe in across such a wide face, and the clefts are too thick to bend in the brake, making it difficult to control the riving.

It is necessary therefore to split the largest poles by using wedges, despite the loss of feel and control that result from their use. After rinding, lay the pole or trunk on the coppice floor, with its thicker end against a stool or a short post firmly driven into the ground. Start riving either by driving a metal wedge centrally into the smaller end with a sledge hammer, or by holding an axe against the end of the pole and smiting its poll with a wooden beetle (fig. 81) – never with a metal sledge.

Once started, continue the split along the pole by driving further wedges in as close to the point of splitting as possible. For the best

81 Splitting large poles: use an axe and beetle to start the split and wedges to continue it

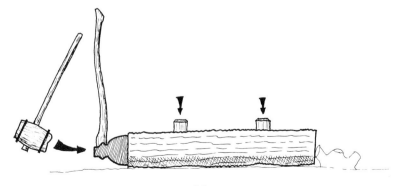

82 *When splitting large segments use round logs to support them*

quality work use hardwood wedges driven by an elm beetle, since they will not leave unsightly torn fibres, bruising, or with oak, the characteristic blue-black stain that results from an interaction between iron and tannin.

If a split starts to wander too far from its line, drive another wedge in along the correct line. This will leave the clefts joined by tongues of wood that must be severed with the axe and finally cleaned off the cleft with a side-axe. Segments can be repeatedly split until the clefts are the size required: to do this support them on two parallel poles, preferably restrained, because to be accurate you must drive the wedges vertically downwards from the circumference (fig. 82).

USING A FROE AND RIVING BRAKE

Millions of gate hurdles and miles of pale and wire fencing have been made from poles riven at a brake or horse. This, together with froe and beetle (*see* Chapter Four) make riving easy. Rest the pole to be cleft at an angle in the brake with its butt on the ground and drive the froe into its end (fig. 83). Then, with the pole held horizontally, lever the froe to left and right to steadily extend the split along its length, progressively moving your tool forward. Do not cut with it unless a knot needs severing, then hit the froe with the beetle actually to cut through it. Sweet poles will require little pressure, and the froe should be held under

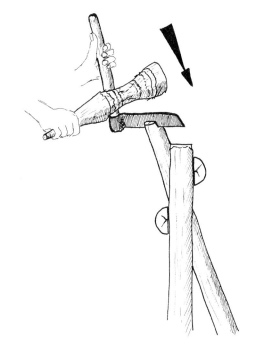

83 *Drive the froe into a pole using a beetle; the pole has its butt on the ground, and is supported by the riving break*

the pole so that no uneven stress is placed on either cleft, which would force the split off-centre. Should this happen anyway, use the spaced horizontal frame of the brake to put the thicker cleft under tension by pressing down on it while working the froe, and the split will return to the centre of the pole (fig. 84).

Halving poles to make gate hurdles is relatively easy. Maximizing the yield of chestnut pales from poles of varying sizes requires more skill, however: a half pole may have to be split into three, or a cleft riven tangentially. To do this you must exert much more care since the two clefts you are producing are of different thicknesses and are much more likely to run out. Avoid applying too much pressure to the clefts or trying to lengthen the split too much with each movement of the froe: a series of quick, short backwards and forwards levering movements gives the best result.

When you have really mastered using the

84 Using a froe to lever a chestnut pole into two clefts. Downward pressure of the left hand can easily apply leverage to centralize the split. The beetle lies to the left of the brake

froe and riving horse, try emulating the trick occasionally performed by Kentish woodmen: take a 150mm(6in) diameter pole about 1.2m (4ft) long and see if you can rive it into 24 or more perfect pales with no waste, which you can then put back together to re-form the pole. If you can do that, you have mastered the art!

HOW TO RIVE SMALL RODS

One of the most skilled techniques in riving is that of cleaving long thin hazel rods accurately and quickly along their entire length using only a billhook. This really is riving by hand, where

the feel and sound of the cleft parting is all, a skill without which you will never make good hurdles or thatching wood.

The simplest method uses a hurdlemaker's billhook or a spar hook. Cut into the rod about 300mm(1ft) from the crown end, penetrating as close to the centre of the rod as possible (fig. 85a). Then twist the hook, pressing the blade face to the rod, to open a split which you then run down the rod by continuing to twist the hook left and right, following your other hand with which you firmly grasp the rod just below the hook (fig. 85b). Use that part of the billhook blade right up by the ferrule, and quick, small levering twists alternately either way. Apply more or less pressure with the back of the hook to either cleft in order to control the direction of the split should it start to wander: bend the thicker cleft more and the split will run towards it.

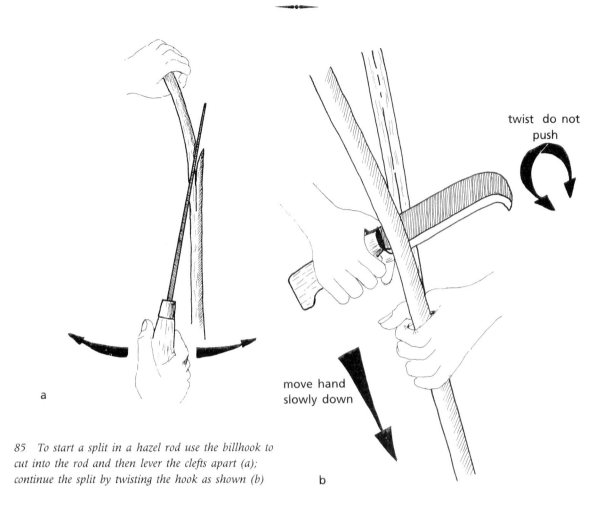

twist do not
push

move hand
slowly down

a

b

*85 To start a split in a hazel rod use the billhook to
cut into the rod and then lever the clefts apart (a);
continue the split by twisting the hook as shown (b)*

Another effective way, particularly for slightly thicker rods, requires a long-nosed riving hook. Stand with your legs slightly apart and staggered, pass a rod between them, and start the split in the way already described. Now extend it along the rod using the nose of the hook to separate the clefts by moving the handle from side to side while keeping the blade as close to the rod as possible, and holding the rod by one of the clefts only (fig. 86). Using the nose of the blade rather than its heel allows you to lever the cleft with much less strain and more control. Should the split start to run out, you simply tension the thicker cleft by bending it to one side whilst it is trapped between your legs. Again, use small levering movements that extend the split by a couple of

inches only with each movement.

Many craftsmen prefer to keep the clefts apart whilst riving by using a *riving post*. This is a 1.2m(4ft) stake driven into the ground with a small peg driven through it which supports the clefts, and which is placed 100mm(4in) below the top (fig. 87). Once you have started a split, open it so that one cleft passes to each side of the post, both resting on the peg. Using your hook to lever the clefts apart, move the rod progressively forward so the post keeps the split well open. In some areas a small adze is used in preference to the billhook, for it offers very controllable leverage to separate the clefts (fig. 87). To use this tool, chop down into the end of the rod to open a split, and progress it by backwards and forwards leverage on the

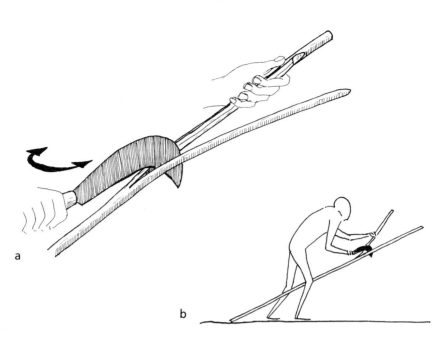

86 To rive long hazel rods use the nose of the billhook to lever the clefts apart (a), and the legs to help apply tension if the split runs off centre (b)

adze. Remember it is solely leverage that you use to separate the clefts, so there is no need to sharpen either side of the blade.

USING THE CLEAVE OR BOND-SPLITTER

Some woodcrafts, such as making bonds for besoms, require very small clefts or *splits*. These are made by splitting rods of only $12\text{mm}(\frac{1}{2}\text{in})$ diameter into three, and to achieve this you

will require a cleave – a three-edged wedge in box or holly wood about the size of an egg (fig. 88). It is unlikely you will ever see a cleave for sale, but they are not difficult to make: turn the basic shape on a lathe, then carefully mark and cut out the three wedges, and you will have a workable cleave. Since even boxwood cannot sever a knot, only use rods that are clean and knot-free. Cut the end of the rod square, and then force the cleave in squarely using a firm pressure (fig. 89a). Progress the

87 Using a small adze together with a riving post to rive a hazel rod

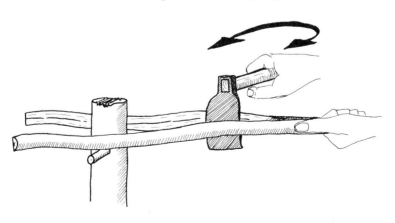

riving by pulling or pushing the cleave steadily down through the rod (fig. 89b), and adjusting the centrality of the split by bending any thicker cleft to tension it.

You can make larger cleaves, up to 230mm (9in) long and with 25mm(1in) or more wide wedges. These are large enough to rive 25mm (1in) diameter rods, and can be used to make broches, or the clefts from which besom bonds are made (*see* Chapter Eleven).

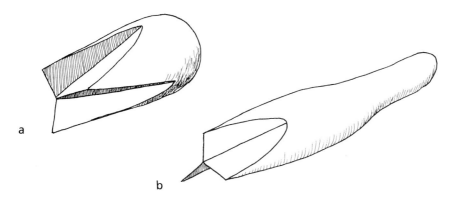

88   Box or holly-wood cleaves: (a) small cleave for hazel rods; (b) larger cleave for ash or oak sticks

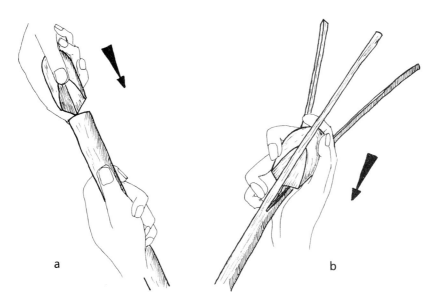

89   Using the cleave: (a) push it into the end of a rod; (b) pull it through a rod to make three clefts

85

CHAPTER · EIGHT

MATERIALS FOR GARDENS AND FENCING

A WEST country wattle hurdle maker tells the story of how his father would never let him make a hurdle until he was 16 years old, some eight years after he started working in the coppice. He spent those eight years trimming rods, cutting pea sticks and making faggots, until his father was happy he had mastered the basic skills.

Preparing products for sale to gardeners (fig. 90) is a good way to learn how to use a billhook and prepare wood, whilst at the same time starting a small market for your produce.

COPPICE PRODUCTS FOR THE GARDEN

THE TOOLS AND MATERIALS REQUIRED

Only the most basic tools are required in order to produce items for sale to gardeners. A billhook is the most essential, but sometimes a bow saw, side-axe or shave will be needed, depending on the size and nature of the product.

Chapter Two described how woodmen traditionally used the different woods growing in the coppice, and garden produce is very much

the province of hazel wood, its size and growth form being ideal. But do not overlook elm, ash, sallow and birch, all of which can produce very saleable product when cut at the right age and properly prepared.

ESTABLISHED PRODUCTS

Bean rods A useable bean rod is a relatively straight clean stick 2.1m(7ft) long and of approximately 25mm(1in) butt diameter. Cut one rod to an exact length as a gauge to measure the remainder. Use your handbill to *thread* all buds and knots flush to the pole by running it up each side.

Discerning customers like their rods sharpened so they go more easily into the ground, and you should do this on a chopping block; four strokes of the side-axe or bill will be sufficient, and aim to leave a 3mm($\frac{1}{8}$in) square point at the tip which will not turn in stony ground.

Bundle your rods in tens or twenties with two bonds, and then store them off the ground on 75mm(3in) poles. Good bean rods are far more wind-resistant than canes when weighted with vines, and finally, when rotten, will warm the gardener's feet.

90 The marvellous productivity of hazel cappice. It includes, from the left: hurdle rods, progs, various stakes, tomato/dahlia stakes, bean rods, tree stakes, lathes, liggers, stakes, broches, morris staves, and pea sticks

Pea sticks It is regrettable that today very few gardeners have the opportunity to appreciate the merits of good pea sticks: apart from providing the perfect support for peas, sweet or otherwise, they can be bent over at a right angle halfway up their length and offer marvellous support against any wind for delphiniums or similar flowers that have grown up through the mat of twigs provided. Laid flat they protect seed beds from cats.

A good pea stick is a flat, fan shaped bough some 1.4m($4\frac{1}{2}$ ft) long, with about 300mm(1ft) of stem at the butt cleaned of twigs (fig. 91), allowing the gardener to erect two close lines of sticks around his peas. Young wood produces the best; put them to one side whilst working up your felled rods, trimming any stray twigs to make them flat. Cut the base obliquely so it pushes into the ground easily.

Bundle 15 or 20 together with one bond, and store them in a *ringe* to flatten them further. A ringe is usually four bundles wide, and you place each subsequent row half on the previous one and half on the ground (fig. 92). Weight the sticks down with a few heavy poles to keep them flat.

Flower stakes Before canes became widely used, every gardener purchased his flower stakes from

91   *Pea stick: flat, fan shaped growth; leave a long pointed stem to push into soil*

the wood. Sold traditionally as flower, dahlia or tomato stakes, they are normally 1.35m(4½ft) long and about 25mm(1in) at the butt. Select nice straight rods, clean them and sharpen them as you would bean rods, and then finally cut the top to an inverted 'V' (fig. 93), with two cuts on the chopping block. This creates the perfect product, for with a 'V' top the stake can be hammered into the ground without splitting.

Finished stakes should be bundled into twenties or twenty-fives.

Crotch sticks or progs   When you work in a wood you will find endless uses for forked sticks and

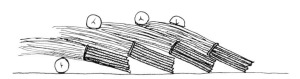

92   *A ringe: lay out bundles of pea sticks weighted wih heavy poles to flatten them*

poles: for making devices, turning-in the fire, or even moving recalcitrant trees. And there is still a good demand for them beyond the wood. Small progs, about 1.2m(4ft) long and 40mm (1½in) diameter are invaluable for supporting the arching boughs of shrubs and other plants on flower beds, whilst larger man-sized ones of 75mm(3in) diameter, known as *lugs* (fig. 94), are still used in orchards to support the laden boughs of fruit trees. Clean any knots from them and sharpen the base.

Clothes props are another good use for forked sticks: 2.4m(8ft) long, straight, about 40mm(1½in) at the butt, and with 15cm(6in) arms. You should give your prop the professional touch by shaving it; this avoids any risk of staining wet garments that touch it. Finally, but perhaps best of all, are fine 1.5m(5ft) dead straight rods that will make thumb sticks – you will sell all you find.

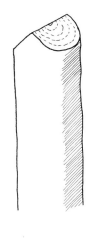 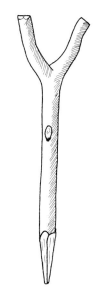

93   (Above left) *Flower stake: cut the top to a 'V' to prevent it spliting when hammered*

94   (Above right) *A lug (or prog): used in various sizes to support fruit trees, shrubs, etc. Cut one side of crotch to be hit with a hammer*

Tree stakes Our modern passion for planting trees has created a useful market for stakes to support them in their early years. For these, cut 65mm($2\frac{1}{2}$in) poles 1.8m(6ft) long, remove all the knots and buds, and using your side-axe sharpen the butt to leave a 6mm($\frac{1}{4}$in) square tip. Chamfer the top to prevent the sides flaking away when hit with a sledge hammer (fig. 95).

Tree stakes are usually rinded only if they are to be treated with preservative: if this is required, use a shaving brake (*see* Chapter Five) and a curved shave to remove the bark.

Rustic poles Most forestry books will say that larch is the stuff of rustic poles, straight and longlasting. But many woodmen would disagree, and chestnut, elm and hazel have been used for many years all over England.

They are never a standard item, since each customer has his own design for rose arbour, pergola or screen, and you will have to cut to the number, size and appearance demanded. For posts to be sunk in the ground use 100mm (4in) diameter wood and shave the butts which seems to lessen rotting. Slimmer poles will suffice for any framework above ground. Be careful when cleaning the poles of knots and branch stubs to remove as little bark as possible, because this is where the elements will

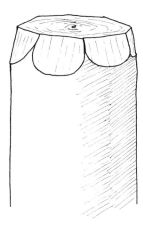

95 *Tree stakes and posts:* champfer *or* half-point *the tops to avoid splitting at the edge when hit*

cause it to peel back in unsightly flakes; and always use winter felled wood, which holds its bark longer.

Hop poles I cannot leave garden produce without mentioning those tall poles raised in hop gardens to support the growing vines. Although largely superseded now by other materials, straight poles 4.8m(16ft) to 6m(20ft) long with a top diameter of 75mm(3in), are used for this job. Ash, lime or chestnut can be used, and should be rinded with a curved shave: support them on two large progs to do this.

FENCING

THE IMPORTANCE OF FENCING

After firewood, fencing in one form or another has always been the greatest user of small wood from the coppice. Although often erected to define estate boundaries or to fence gardens, restraining livestock in an increasingly ordered countryside created the major demand. The Normans enclosed their deer parks within a wooden *pale*, and many estates still retain the remnants of their park pale; wherever sheep, cattle and horses are kept, fencing is needed, and even barbed wire needs *spiles* to support it. Even today pale and wire remains the cheapest quick fence for any purpose.

In some regions the demand for fencing has reduced with the loss of both animals and hedgerows from farmland, but a resurgence of interest in managing woodlands coupled with an increasing wild deer population may halt this decline (fig. 96).

TOOLS AND MATERIALS REQUIRED

Most fencing is straightforward to prepare. In addition to the basic tools needed to fell and trim up your poles, a froe, beetle and side-axe are essential for making cleft or sharpened product. Suitable brakes for riving wood have been covered in Chapter Five.

96 *Chestnut pale and wire fencing, still a major coppice product. Here 1.8m(6ft) fencing is being used to stop deer from browsing a cant within a woodland*

As we have seen, chestnut is the supreme wood for fencing. But do not underestimate the value of ash for rails and even pales when clear of the ground, and use hazel, not chestnut, for hedging material.

STAKES AND ETHERS FOR HEDGING

Increasing awareness of the hedgerow's importance in our countryside, backed in some cases by grants to the landowner, has kept alive traditional methods of managing them. *Laying* a hedge is perhaps the most important of these,

a process in which young stems are part cut through and layed at an angle to form a dense, stock proof hedge. To accomplish this a large number of stakes is required, which together with long thin *ethering* rods hold the layered stems in place (fig. 97).

Cut the stakes from any reasonably straight 50mm(2in) diameter wood to a length of 1.5m(5ft), although individual customers may prefer them longer or shorter. Clean off any knots, and if required, sharpen with your side-axe, although most hedgers prefer to sharpen their own.

The ethering rods (also called *heathering rods* or *binders*) that go with the stakes are thin rods of hazel, up to 3.6m(12ft) long and about 38mm(1½in) butt diameter. Trim off any side branches as you would bean rods, making sure

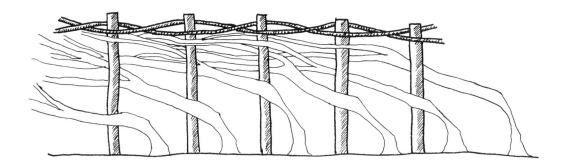

97 Stakes and ethers: stakes are driven between laid stems of a hedge, and ethers are then wound between them to hold the laid stems in place

not to cut into the stem which could then break when woven between the stakes. Bundle 25 rods together, and store them off the ground and in shade.

FENCING PRODUCTS

Spiles These may be cleft or round, rinded or bark on, sharpened or not, but are invariably 1.6m(5½ft) long and approximately 75mm(3in) in diameter or across the cleft face.

Cut your poles to length, use your side-axe to remove any knots, and then if required, rind them on a brake similar to that shown in fig. 59. Larger poles should be riven: 100mm(4in) ones into two; 150mm(6in) ones into four, and so on. After riving, clean up the cleft faces with a side-axe, removing any sharp spears which have been raised.

Many spiles today are sharpened on the saw bench, but you can still do this with your sideaxe (*see* Chapter Four). Two key points to remember when sharpening a post are first, to leave a small square at the tip, and secondly not to make the point too blunt (fig. 98), because then it will not drive easily.

Stack your finished spiles in criss-cross layers, clear of the ground.

Posts Where spiles serve for any light fencing work around the farm or small holding, posts are heavier, designed to take the strain of tensioned wire or to support stout rails. Though normally longer than 1.6m(5½ft) and thicker than 100mm(4in) they should be prepared in the same way. Large posts are infrequently sharpened, since they are usually dug into the ground, not driven.

Square posts mortised to accommodate rails were once hewn in the wood using axe and adze, but are now usually prepared at the woodyard where they are more easily shaped on a sawbench. The arrival of chainsaws modified for planking round wood does now mean that sqare posts could be produced in the coppice; if you do, remember this type of post should be cut about 130mm(5in) square with a sloping top (fig. 99) to shed rain, which means

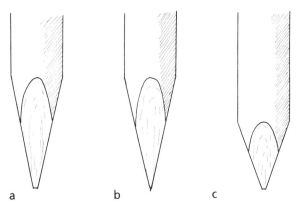

98 Pointing stakes: (a) is correct – shoulder well back and small flat at tip; (b) incorrect – feather point that will turn when driven; (c) incorrect – shoulder too close to point, stake hard to drive into ground

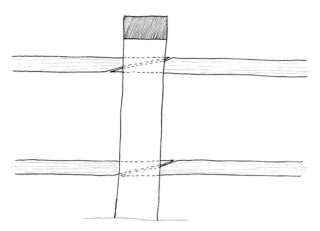

99   Post and rail fence: angle the top of the post to shed water and slope ends of rails so they overlap in the mortice

it cannot be driven and should therefore not be sharpened.

Gateposts were similarly hewn from the round, but to a size often of 200mm(8in) square and with a conical top (fig. 100). A traditional gatepost's most important feature is out of sight: the 900mm(3ft) below ground that is left in the round to provide a solid, firm base. Unfortunately posts are hard work to prepare and even harder to sell against modern tanalized softwood versions.

Rails   A considerable amount of fencing consists of posts joined by two rails, sometimes to which pales are nailed. Because they are clear of the ground, these rails can be of less durable material than the posts, and both ash and hazel frequently provide the 2.4–3m(8–10ft) straight lengths required. Rive fence rails from 75mm (3in) diameter poles, cleaning up the cleft faces and removing the bark with a draw-knife. You may be asked to taper the last 150mm(6in), since it is usual to overlap the rails within the mortice (fig. 99): do this with your side-axe.

Feather-edge pales   These pales are broad flat clefts approximately 75–100mm(3–4in) wide and varying in length, although 1.06m($3\frac{1}{2}$ft) is

very common. They are radial clefts from a round pole, and so are thinner or *feather-edged* at their innermost point (fig. 101a). In fact they are rarely thinner than 6mm($\frac{1}{4}$in) at this edge.

To make pales, select fairly straight poles, cut them to the required length, and rind them. Then, using froe and brake, rive the pole into progressively smaller clefts: halves; quarters; eighths; etc. Aim for a final outside edge thickness on your pale of 12–19mm($\frac{1}{2}$–$\frac{3}{4}$in), so that a 150mm(6in) diameter pale should give between 24 and 36 pales depending on the quality of the wood and your skill (fig. 102). The innermost edge of your clefts will feather away to nothing, and this should be trimmed back to about 6mm($\frac{1}{4}$in) thick. Depending on the quality specified by your customer you may be able to use curved pales from the butt of the pole; but bear in mind pales are usually nailed to their rails at not much more than 75mm(3in) spacing, so if the curve will exceed this, trim it back with your side-axe (fig. 101b).

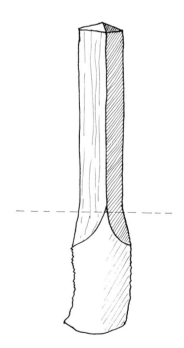

100   A traditional gate post shaped from a round trunk which is left intact underground

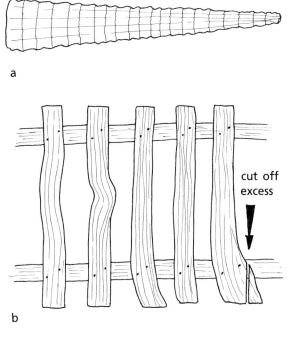

101 Feather edge pales: (a) cross section of finished pale; (b) pales nailed to rails; note how you must trim badly mis-shapen ones to maintain an even spacing

Green wood clefts have a habit of warping as they dry, so it is best to bundle them soon after riving.

Cleft chestnut pale fencing Making pale and wire fencing is still an industry in the southern counties of England. Most people are familiar with this fencing made of small clefts of wood held at spaced intervals by two or more rows of twisted wires (fig. 96). It is seen around building sites, parks and gardens throughout the land, and if kept 50mm(2in) or so off the ground as it is designed to be, will last 20 years or more. The pales are always riven from sweet chestnut, the only tree with sufficient heart-wood to make durable clefts in such small sizes. The product is governed by a British Standard (Number 1722, part four, for those who are going to take it seriously!).

Pale and wire comes in a variety of sizes from 600mm(2ft) to 1.8m(6ft), and with the

pales set at spacings of 25mm(1in) up to 125mm(5in) depending on the application. Pales for all sizes are produced the same way. After cutting your poles to length and shaving them, use your froe and brake to cleave them into roughly triangular palings with a cleft face of between 25mm(1in) and 44mm($1\frac{3}{4}$in). Small round rods can simply be halved, slightly larger ones quartered, and so on (fig. 102) until you reach a 150mm(6in) pole from which 24 pales are possible. Go gently with the froe, for if you lever too strongly these small clefts will easily split out and leave you with a pile of waste.

After riving, bluntly sharpen each paling at one end (fig. 103) with three strokes of your side-axe or handbill. Normally the pales are delivered in bundles of 25 to a factory which produces the fencing. Use a notch (fig. 58) to

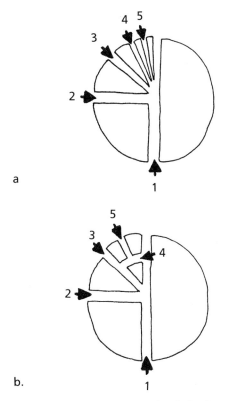

102 Riving patterns: (a) sequence of radial splits to make feather edged pales; (b) sequence of radial and tangential splits to make pale and wire fencing

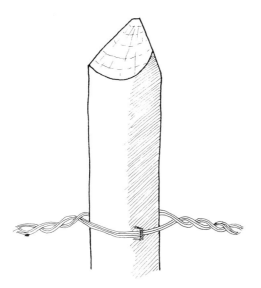

103 Pale and wire fencing: sharpen top of pale to a blunt point, staple wire to pale, then twist wire in alternate direction after every pale

remains of a fence-maker's pitch may still be found under the leaves in neglected chestnut coppices. Fig. 104 shows the simplest method, using two poles about 5m(17ft) apart. The two 14-gauge wires for each strand are kept taut by passing them through the tension arms fixed to one post, and by simply wrapping them around the other. Insert a paling between the paired wires of each strand, and using a grooved 300mm(1ft) bar, twist the wires three times one way; insert another paling and twist the wires three times in the opposite direction. Continue inserting palings and twisting alternately to right or left, and to avoid the palings slipping out, fix them to the wire with small staples. Cut the wire at the tensioned end after a final twist, roll up the length from this end, and use the surplus wire pulled back through the post at the other end to secure the bundle. Pale and wire fencing should always be erected pointed end uppermost.

tie your bundles so that they are tight enough to prevent the pales from warping.

In the factory the process of wiring the pales together is done mechanically, using two strands for short fencing, and three for large. It can be made in the wood, however, and the

104 Device to make pale and wire fencing in the wood: feed wire through holes in posts and tie at starting post (a); use metal brackets to tension the wire at the other end (b), pulling them down with weights to increase the tension if necessary

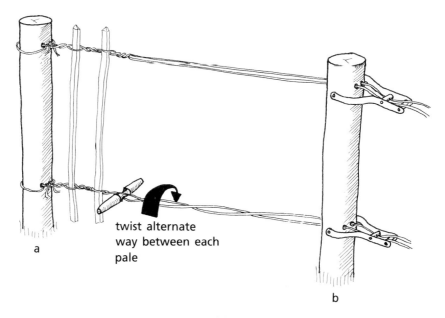

twist alternate way between each pale

a

b

CHAPTER · NINE

THATCHING WOOD

Shortly before he died in 1985, a Suffolk gate hurdle and broche maker gave me a photograph taken at the 1960 Royal Show that depicts him sharpening three foot long rick pegs with his Suffolk billhook. Although the thatching of corn ricks was even then unusual, and is now a rarity, thatching wood for cottage roofs is still an important market for hazel wood.

ABOUT THATCH

A BRIEF HISTORY

Thatching is the oldest of the building crafts. Before fired tiles, stone or slate became widely available, the most suitable local vegetation including reed, sedge, heather and bracken were used to roof hovels and houses. With the exception of coastal reed, which remains the most durable of all, these were gradually supplanted by straw from the wheatlands, which in turn increased the demand for thatchers, since corn ricks needed thatching until they could be threshed.

By the Middle Ages thatching was an established craft whose work was clearly recorded in the documents of the day. And it is here that we find the first references to *broches*, *spars* and *ledgers* – the wood required to fix the thatch.

Where wheat and reed thrive and thatched roofs are part of the vernacular architecture, thatching remains a living craft. In my own county of Suffolk, Kelly's Directory for 1900 listed 82 thatchers; today an active Master Thatchers' Association has 20 members, and there are nearly 1000 nationally, sustained by both the merits of good thatch and the planners regulations. And despite flirtations with plastic alternatives, a majority of them still use hazel wood to hold and decorate the outer layers of their thatch.

THE ROLE OF WOOD IN THATCHING

Small wood has been traditionally used in various roles to hold the thatching material. *Sways* or *binders* are round or cleft lengths, 1.5m(5ft) to 2.4m(8ft) long and about 25mm (1in) across, which are used with metal hooks to hold the underthatch to the rafters. *Liggers* or *runners* are 1m(3ft) to 1.5m(5ft) long lengths cleft from 38mm(1½in) rods, and are seen outside the thatch securing it at ridge and eaves. Liggers may be cut down to make the *cross rods*

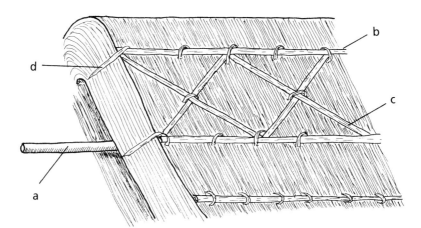

105 Thatching wood on a roof: sway (a) holding underthatch; liggers (b) and cross rods (c) holding ridge; and broches (d) pegging these rods to the thatch

that criss-cross between the liggers on the ridge (fig. 105).

The straw or reed used at the eaves is tied into bundles called *bottles*, and the binding for these was frequently 12mm($\frac{1}{2}$in) rods twisted to make *withes*. Nowadays tarred twine has replaced these small hazel or willow rods.

Finally, liggers, cross rods and some of the underthatch are held in place by *broches* (fig. 106) – thin cleft rods about 12mm($\frac{1}{2}$in) across, twisted to make a hairpin which is driven into the thatch with a mallet. Broche is a Suffolk name; in Essex they are *springles*; in Dorset *spars*; in Wiltshire *stakes* or *spits*... almost every county it seems has its own term for these small clefts. They are normally cut 660mm(26in) long, although some thatchers do prefer them at 760mm(30in). But whatever their name or size, a remarkable number is used: every 10m sq(100ft sq) of thatch uses 400; every 300mm (1ft) of ridge uses 50. So thatching one roof alone requires between six and twelve thousand broches (fig. 107), and the annual demand in England is currently estimated at twenty million!

Thatching wood is invariably hazel, for it is easy to use and is the most durable. This was not always so: willow or sallow were frequently used as substitutes, and although coppice wood grows sweetest, that from other sites was used, as shown by Richard Jefferies' description of a Wiltshire thatcher in 1879 splitting his stakes '... of willow, cut from the pollard trees by the brook...'.*

Like woodmen, thatchers prefer their wood cut when sapdrained – December to February – since then it contains least water and hence lasts longer and works more easily. Each spring most thatchers purchase sufficient round wood

106 A broche sharpened and twisted into a hairpin ready for use

* Richard Jefferies, *Wild Life in a Southern County*, Smith, Elder & Co., 1879

96

*107 Broches sharpened and bundled with withes
ready for delivery to the thatcher. This remains one of
the most important outlets for underwood*

to last a full twelve months, working it up
themselves into liggers, sways and broches
when bad weather prevents work upon the
roof. Specialist broche makers also buy rods
and then sell what they have made to the

thatchers. That the broches dry out matters little
since a good dousing in a tub of water restores
sufficient suppleness to allow them to be twisted
to the necessary hairpin. Finally many woodmen, seeking to keep themselves employed
beyond the cutting season without resort to
labouring, work up their own rods to meet the
summer demand, swelled in dog days past by
the need of rick pegs for haysel (hay-making)
and harvest.

PREPARING WOOD FOR THATCHERS

WOOD IN THE ROUND

Preparing round hazel rods for sale to thatchers or broche makers is straightforward, but requires care. Put aside suitable material whilst working up your felled wood: it should be fairly straight, no shorter than 1.3m(4ft 6in) and you must carefully clean off major knots and branches without baring the sapwood, which will create sere patches. And do not use sere wood, damaged wood, wood grown round entwining honeysuckle, or badly gnawed or barked rods since they will not rive cleanly nor produce usable product. Thatchers will take a wide range of wood, but prefer the different sizes clearly separated, for each will be used for a specific job. Bundle rods from 12mm($\frac{1}{2}$in) to 25mm(1in), and from 25mm(1in) to 50mm (2in) diameter separately, and also those less than six feet long. Tie them in bundles of 20 or 25 with two withes or lengths of twine, and then store them clear of the ground either across lengths of cord wood or, if only a few, standing on their butts against a timber tree adjacent to the ride.

BROCHES

To make broches yourself it is best to collect, grade and store your wood as described in the last section, for it may be June or July before you rive it down. A store of broche wood will stand you in good stead against those winter days when weather makes even the coppice unworkable, for then you can retire to a shed or ruder shelter and rive it down in relative comfort.

Prime broche wood is between 25mm(1in) and 50mm(2in) diameter, but real masters of the craft can rive 20 or more perfect broches from a 63mm($2\frac{1}{2}$in) rod. One thatcher recounts how, when untying a bundle of broches one day, he found a smaller bundle in the centre and written along the cleft face of one broche were the words 'These 24 broches were split from one piece of wood by Frank Linnet'. Fresh cut rods are often too tender to rive that well except perhaps in a cold early January, so give them time to 'toughen up' a little; most woodmen did not start working up their thatching wood until May or June when their wattle hurdle making was finished for the season.

The first job is to cut your rods into *gads* from which the broches will be riven. Cut each gad 25mm(1in) longer than the finished broche you require to allow for a little loss when sharpening, and only from straight, knot-free wood. Saw your gads on a horse to which a measuring rod is attached (fig. 108) so that every one is the same length.

108 Cutting gads: use a measuring rod on the sawing horse to gauge the length of each gad

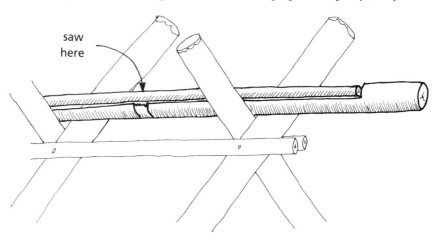

saw
here

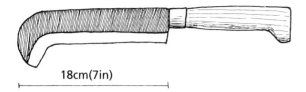

109 *Spar hook: a small hook used to rive gads and sharpen broches*

Woodmen rive broches the way their fathers and grandfathers did, often using the very same tool: some use a small adze and riving post; others prefer a billhook; whilst most thatchers use a *spar hook* – a small-bladed billhook (fig. 109).

The principles of riving small rods were explained in Chapter Seven, but you can hone up your broche making by using the methods already perfected by the experts. Suffolk woodmen use a *riving stool* (fig. 110). Built on three or four legs, it is fitted at the front with a pole, a part of which is sharpened to a 'V' with shoulders at its base to support the split

gad. Once you have opened a split using adze or hook, you use the 'V' wedge on the post to keep it open as you rive along the gad. This works extremely well and an experienced man can make 1600 broches in a day using this method.

It is more usual to use the spar hook alone, without the help of the horse. To start, rest a gad vertically on a convenient log or block (fig. 111), and begin a split by forcing your hook into the end. Then, holding the gad under your arm, lever the clefts apart by twisting the hook (fig. 112). Sitting in the warm May sun, this is possibly the nicest job in the wood.

Finished broches should have a cleft face between 13–19mm($\frac{1}{2}$–$\frac{3}{4}$in), and this determines how each gad must be riven. A 25mm (1in) gad should be quartered; a 38mm($1\frac{1}{2}$in) gad riven into six, and from a 50mm(2in) gad you should aim to get sixteen broches

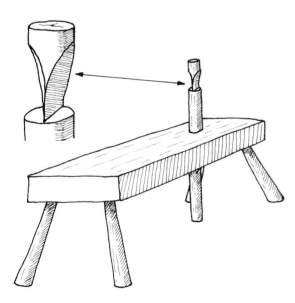

110 *Riving stool: stool used in Suffolk for making broches; use the 'V' post to separate the clefts during riving*

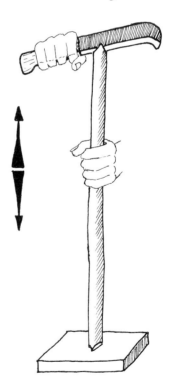

111 *When riving gads start a split with the spar hook by banging the gad on a block*

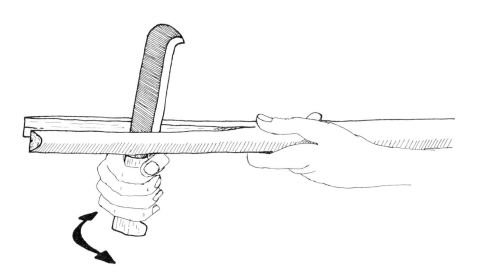

112   Riving gads: use the spar hook to lever the clefts apart; hold the other end of the gad firmly under the left arm

(fig. 113). Then, when you have really mastered the craft, see if you can get 20 or 24 from a 63mm(2½in) gad! As the rods increase in size, so will the pile of waste wood, unless you exercise sufficient care when riving a piece into thirds or splitting wood tangentially, because the differing stiffness of either cleft means they will *run-out* more easily. Use your hook to clean any rough spears from the finished broche.

To collect your finished broches, set up beside your riving stool a simple device of two horizontal poles and four short posts (fig. 114), and when you have sufficient, bind them into bundles of 100 or 200 using two withes or lengths of twine. You can use a woodman's grip to compress them first (*see* Chapter Five), but however tight a bond you make it cannot defy the laws of nature: cleft wood shrinks as it dries, and 200 broches shrink by a measurable amount resulting in slack bundles. To overcome this problem undercount each bundle by three, and then shortly before they are collected by the thatcher, force in these last three broches to make the bundle tight.

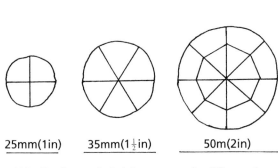

25mm(1in)   35mm(1½in)   50m(2in)

113   Broches: typical riving patterns for different sizes of gad producing respectively four, six and sixteen broches

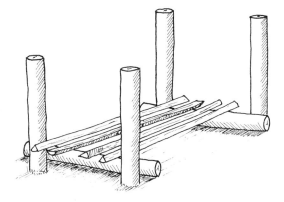

114   A simple device for collecting broches which makes it easy to bundle 100 together

Most broches are sold unsharpened since they store better in this form. If they are to be used immediately your thatcher may prefer them sharpened. To do this sit comfortably and place a protective piece of leather or the split top of an old wellington boot across your right thigh. Hold a broche firmly across this (fig. 115), and pressing your right elbow well in to the body, make a quick cut with the spar hook using mainly wrist and a little forearm movement to remove a chip from the end. Rotate the broche, make another cut, and repeat once more to produce a sharpened end (fig. 116). Three strokes at the correct angle will produce a sharp firm point; avoid a flexible *feather* point that will turn when forced into the thatch. Once practised you should be able to sharpen 250 an hour.

RICK PEGS

In far off summers when hay and corn were held in ricks, thousands of *pegs* or spars were needed to thatch them. In East Anglia 1.06m(3ft 6in) long *rick pegs* were used; in the southern counties there were *hay spars* 910mm(3ft) long (sometimes more descriptively called *yard spars*), and *corn spars* which were 1.2m(4ft). These long pegs are driven into the ricks to secure the twine that holds the thatching layer against autumn wind and rain. Because they are not twisted, pegs are thicker than broches, about 25mm(1in) diameter, either round or cleft, and cut from hazel, elm, willow, ash, lime or even maple. Each peg is sharpened at one end only, the other being used to drive it home.

If you find a call for rick pegs, make them from wood left over after more important produce has been selected out, the wood that has no other use. You can size, rive, sharpen and bundle rick pegs the same way as broches. Due to their larger size and weight, only bundle 100 pegs together, putting any bent ones in the centre where they will be straightened out.

LIGGERS OR RUNNERS

These are invariably made by thatchers themselves. But if asked, make them as follows. Cut knot-free lengths of hazel to the size required and rive them into four clefts. Clean from the cleft faces any spears or threads, trim out the

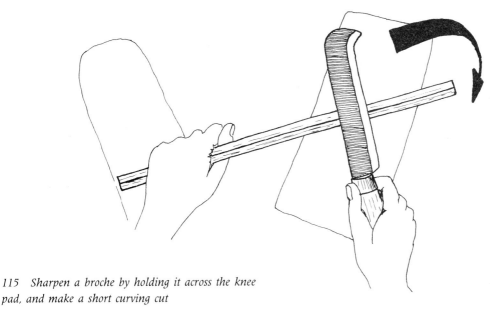

115   *Sharpen a broche by holding it across the knee pad, and make a short curving cut*

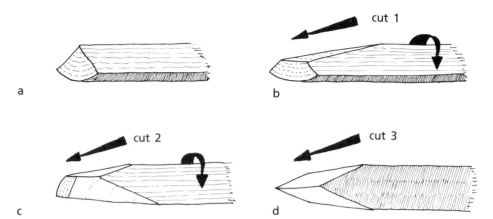

a

cut 1

b

cut 2

c

cut 3

d

pithy centre to give a flat face, and finally shape both ends to a 100mm(4in) long taper. When flattening the centre take note of any wind in the cleft, and trim each end differently to avoid a twisted end product. Tie 25 finished liggers with two withes, and store them dry whilst awaiting collection.

SWAYS OR BINDERS

To make these use either straight, round rods or riven wood produced as described for liggers but without shaping, for being under the thatch neat joining of the ends is less important.

116 Sharpen by making three cuts, one to each corner, rotating the broche between each one; make a short but sharp point

CHAPTER · TEN

A MISCELLANY
OF PRODUCTS

THE number of products fashioned from small round wood is seemingly endless, because coppice workers have increasingly had to innovate in order to dispose of all their wood. Producing a range of products has never been more important than today, when so many of the customary markets are at a low ebb.

In this chapter we shall consider first the way some of the less obvious commodities are made using methods that you can easily adapt to make other novel or original artefacts, then material you can prepare for other craftsmen, and finally how to dispose of the cordwood and offal from the cut.

FROM TENT PEGS TO WITHES

TENT PEGS

Over fifty million tent pegs were produced during the last war, and cleft wooden pegs still sell in hundreds of thousands each year to the services, campers and marquee erectors, mainly because they grip the ground better than metal pegs. Sizes vary from 150mm(6in) to 610mm(2ft), although the basic pattern (fig. 117) remains similar. Ash and chestnut poles

of at least 150mm(6in) diameter make the best.

You will need saw, froe, draw-knife and a sit-on shaving horse (drawing horse) in order to make pegs (fig. 118). Cut your roundwood to the length of peg required, discarding any knotty dog-legs, and then split it radially into segments sized for the peg, i.e. about 19mm ($\frac{3}{4}$in) thick at the circumference for a 300mm (12in) peg. Shave back the feather edge until it is about 6mm($\frac{1}{4}$in) thick, and at a point about one quarter the total length from one end, make a saw cut 19mm($\frac{3}{4}$in) deep and angled as shown to form the top of the notch (fig. 117a). Now complete the shaping of the peg using horse and knife. Shave a nice curve back from the centre of the blade to the base of the notch cut, chamfering the edges for smoothness; shape the bottom half of the blade to a point, leaving a 3mm($\frac{1}{8}$in) square tip; and then curve the head back from the notch and chamfer it, to avoid it splitting when driven (fig. 117). Stack your finished pegs two by two to season.

LATHES AND WATTLE RODS

Small wood has been used for centuries in house building either as round wattle rods fitted between the beams of timber framed houses to

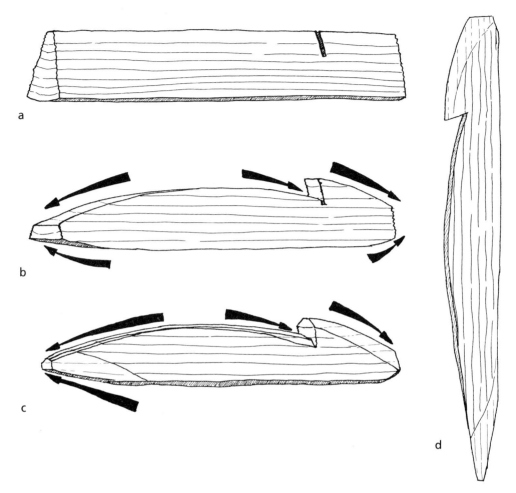

a

b

c

d

117   Tent pegs: (a) a cleft ready for shaping;
(b) shaping the peg – always cut with the grain;
(c) champfering the edges and pointing;
(d) the finished peg

hold the daub which made each wall panel or as clefts nailed to the ceiling joists to hold plaster. Although modern house construction has no need of either, there is a small but steady sale to builders who renovate old houses.

Wattle rods are simply hazel rods about 13mm($\frac{1}{2}$in) diameter, cleaned up and cut to any length between 900mm(3ft) and 1.8m(6ft) as specified by the user.

Lathes are cleft. Start with clean, straight rods already cut to length (normally 900mm (3ft), of 50–75mm(2–3in) diameter, and using a froe, cleave them in half. Then carefully rive from each half, clefts about 9mm($\frac{3}{8}$in) thick to form the final lathes (fig. 119). Do not clean them up, for the rough surface left by riving helps any plaster to adhere, but discard the two outermost bark-covered clefts. When you have made two dozen, bind them tightly so that they do not warp too much as they dry.

STAVES

The good thing about supplying staves to morris dancers is that their heavy use ensures a steady demand. To make them, cut 38mm(1$\frac{1}{2}$in) poles to a length of 900mm(3ft), making sure they are dead straight. Carefully remove any buds flush with the bark, and you have the stave that some groups require.

Most prefer their staves shaved (fig. 90). To do this it is best to use a small sit-on horse. Remove the bark and any buds with a draw-knife, and then smooth the stave using a small shave as described in Chapter Four. To avoid radial splits occurring along the length of the stave after shaving, season them for three months before working on them, and then allow them to dry slowly under cover.

118 Peggers at work using their shaving horses. Note the metal strips inserted into the vice on their horses to grip the pegs, and how they tighten the vice by pushing with their legs

119 How to split lathes from a round pole; the top and bottom clefts are waste

BARREL HOOPS

Time was when almost everything was conveyed in *slack barrels*, from fish to fruit, from flour to cement. Unlike their iron-bound watertight brethren, the looser staves of slack barrels were bound with wooden *hoops* made in the copse (fig. 120). Today, very few slack barrels are made, and those mainly in halves for use as flower tubs. But should you need to, make hoops this way.

You will need billhook, adze or froe, a shaving horse, and possibly a coiling device. Cut straight 38mm – 63mm($1\frac{1}{2}$–$2\frac{1}{2}$in) rods free from major branches and knots, to between 2.1m(7ft) and 1.2m(4ft), depending on the barrel size. Remove the buds carefully, because any cut may well split open when the cleft is bent into a hoop. Then using adze or froe rive them into four triangular clefts at least 25mm(1in) across. Each cleft must now be shaved to leave it 13mm($\frac{1}{2}$in) thick, using draw-knife and knee-operated shaving horse (fig. 121). It is essential to maintain an even

thickness, for any thin points will fold instead of curving when flexed into a hoop.

Straight hoops are bundled in 60s, sufficient for ten barrels, but must be soaked before use to make them supple. To avoid this problem, most hoop-makers coiled hoops whilst the wood was green and pliable. To do this you need a device made with two rollers (fig. 122) so arranged that you can lever the cleft to a curve as you push it between them. After coiling the first hoop, its *scarfed* ends must be nailed together. Coil another five hoops and fit these, without nailing, inside the first hoop to make a set for one barrel, and then tie all six together with two ties, ready for immediate use.

120 A barrel hoop. The cross section shows how the inside of the cleft should be shaved smooth, and the bark left on the outside. Both ends have been scarfed and must be nailed together

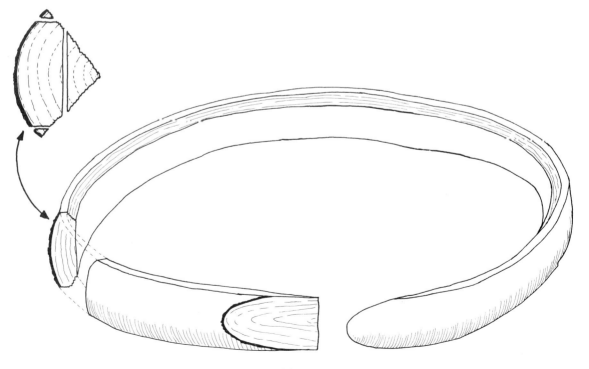

121 (Above) *Shaving barrel hoops: this type of horse offers a long bed on which to shave the clefts, making it easier to keep an even thickness. Beside the horse is a frame to hold cleft rods*

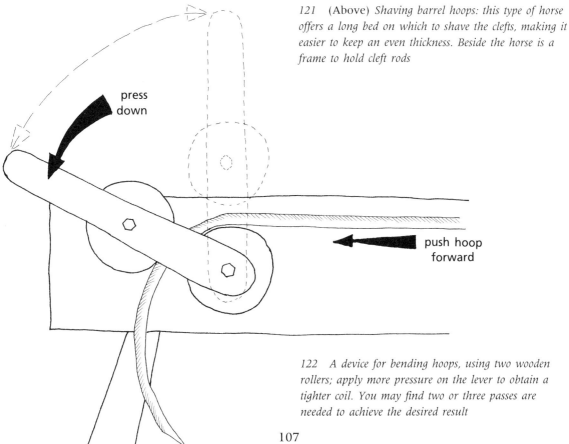

press down

push hoop forward

122 *A device for bending hoops, using two wooden rollers; apply more pressure on the lever to obtain a tighter coil. You may find two or three passes are needed to achieve the desired result*

WITHES OR BONDS

For centuries woodmen obtained their bindings from the wood, using everything from lime bast to bindweed. But it is *withes* or *bonds*, thin hardwood rods twisted to make a 'rope', that have stood the test of time better than any other, and although nylon baler twine is now more common, many woodmen still use them (see figs. 33 and 107, pages 48 and 97).

To understand the principle of making a withe, think of a hazel rod as a bundle of threads held together by the bark. To make a loop or noose with the rod without it breaking, these threads must be separated and twisted, like the strands of a rope (fig. 123a). This is accomplished by *winding* the rod. Thread a 19mm($\frac{3}{4}$ in) diameter, 1.5m(5ft) long rod of its knots and buds, being careful not to nick it. Hold the butt end under your foot with the rod curving up to your hands, grasp the end firmly and twist it until you hear and feel the fibres part (fig. 124). Wind the rod three or four times – no more or it will break – then work the fibres apart along its whole length by winding it vigorously as if pedalling by hand, moving one hand along the rod as you go.

124 *Winding a withe: note how the rod is being wound whilst it is held in a curve with one end underfoot*

a

123 *The withe: (a) shows how the fibres in a rod separate when it is twisted, (b) a withe showing the running loop 'x' and the final knot 'y' with the end tucked away*

Once the fibres are separated from top to bottom, wind the top some more and it will naturally form a running loop. To use the withe pass its butt end around your product, through the loop, and pull hard on it. Twist the free end again and it will naturally form a small loop or knot which locks the withe (fig. 123b), and then poke the end away into the bundle. Withes do not slacken or break, and so good were they that crate-makers re-used those with which their rods were tied.

These days you will probably use string or twine more often than withes to tie your material. There are many ways of doing this, but the method explained in figure 125 allows the twine to be pulled really tight, to be knotted without slackening, and to be re-used.

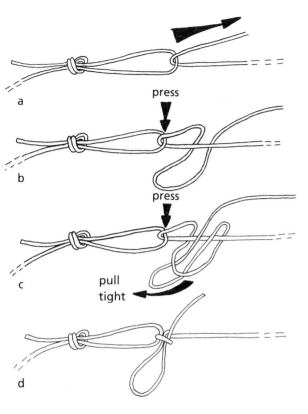

125   *Method for tying a knot with twine: (a) pull the bond tight; (b) and (c) press down as shown to keep the bond taught whilst tying the knot; (d) the finished knot, which is easily released by pulling the free end of the twine*

Supplying Materials for Other Craftsmen

Wood can be sold direct to craftsmen or rural factories. Most have unwritten specifications which differ with each use or establishment; get to know those in your locality.

CRATE RODS

Crates were extremely large basket-like containers made largely from hazel, in which china was transported, often as much as one ton at a time. For nearly two hundred years, the potteries used thousands of crates, but by the 1990s only a couple of crate-makers were still working and the craft, once a user of millions of hazel rods, is almost dead.

Rods for crate-making are very carefully selected. They should be sorted into '20s' – approx 50mm(2in) by 3m(10ft) long; '40s' – approx 32mm($1\frac{1}{4}$in) by 3m(10ft) long; '75s' – approx 12mm($\frac{1}{2}$in) by any length; and finally '100s' or *jimps* for withes at 13mm($\frac{1}{2}$in) by 2.1m(7ft) long. Each number defines both the type of rod and the number in a bundle. Any rods that have been cut or nicked during cleaning up are useless to the crate-makers, who require only the finest hazel. For many years the coppices around Basingstoke in Hampshire have alone been able to supply them.

HANDLES

Straight clean poles have always been prized as handles. Richard Jefferies suggested that when 'poles cut from copses' were added to a billhook, the resulting weapon was 'irresistible'.* But it was agriculture that created an enormous demand, for every rake, scythe, hoe, pitchfork, beetle and broom required a tough straight-grained handle that could only be made from a small pole, steamed and straightened by a craftsman.

Only axe and billhook are needed to fell and clean the poles, which are best cut at 12–15 years when 50–75mm(2–3in) at the butt. Discard those that are sere, dog-legged or hopelessly knotted. Then sort them by length and species to the customary requirements, which are: 2.1m(7ft) long for scythe *snaiths*, separated into ash alone for American pattern, but adding sallow and alder for others; 1.8m(6ft) long for rake *stails* in ash, sallow or hazel; other handles 1.8m(6ft) long of any wood. Alder and birch are termed 'soft' woods, and you must remove two or three *blazes* of bark along their length soon after felling in order

---

* Richard Jefferies, *Chronicles of the Hedges*, Phoenix, 1948

126 A 'dolly' shave, used to remove strips of bark from poles. No brake is required, just hold the pole vertically and run the shave down over it

that they season properly without rotting. Use your draw-knife and a simple green wood vice and prog (fig. 63), to do this. A Kentish woodman devised a unique tool with a semi-circular cutting edge which performs this task with ease, and eliminates the need for the vice (fig. 126).

Either despatch or cover ash poles before the bark beetle burrows into them in early summer.

TURNERY

Broom or *dolly* factories have always taken large numbers of poles up to 250mm(10in) diameter for conversion into cheap brooms, brushes and similar goods. They use much birch and alder, species less useful to the woodman for other crafts, and they are less demanding over quality than rake and scythe stick makers. These, together with the few factories that still turn bobbins from round wood, may provide a useful market, but be sure you understand their requirements before you start.

WALKING-STICKS

As you work your wood you will always find some sticks suitable for the walking-stick craftsman. Put them to one side as you see them. Those which have a spirally deformed

growth along their length caused by entwining honeysuckle are the most valuable, but species with opposed buds often give the perfect fork for a thumb-stick; dogwood and ash are particularly good. This is also the best use for young blackthorn stems. Always cut the sticks longer than required, and remember that knots or lumps at one end can be attractively shaped by a good stick maker.

USES FOR CORDWOOD AND BRASH

FAGGOTS FOR FUEL

'A bundle of sticks or twigs bound together as fuel', is how the dictionary defines a *faggot* (fig. 127a). Made from the real offal of the cut, those sticks with no craft use at all, they fuelled countrymen's hearths, baker's ovens, and brewer's maltings. And in the wider country-side faggots found other uses too: as a base to corn and hay stacks; laid in ditches instead of pipes since water percolated freely through them; and staked on river banks or tidal marshes to prevent erosion. Although faggots are very rarely used for firing these days, they still find use in coastal and river defence, and a good billhook with a long curved blade, often called a *faggoting hook*, is all you need to prepare them.

Making faggots Evelyn tells us a proper faggot is 'a full yard long (900mm) and two feet (610mm) in circumference', and that it should be 'every stick of three feet long . . . to prevent the abuse of filling the middle with brash and short sticks'.* Since the seventeenth century standards have declined somewhat, and it is now common to put some sere wood and twigs in the centre of the faggot to get it blazing well!

To make a faggot, drive two 900mm(3ft)

---

* John Evelyn, *Sylva, or a discourse on forest trees*, (ed. J. Hunter), London, 1786

b

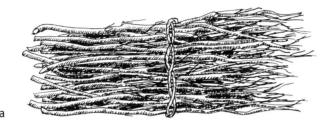

a

posts into the ground 450mm(18in) apart (fig. 128). Lay between these two or three pieces of well-branched brushwood cut to length, then follow them with a mixture of sticks and brushwood from the slays left after working up. Trim up any pieces that are too large or straggly, lay the butts to one end, and pile sufficient to give a 450mm(18in) diameter, roughly held by the two posts. Finish it by tying it once around the middle with a withe or twine.

127 Faggots: (a) shows the traditional faggot for fuelling ovens, (b) a longer type, or fascine, still used in large quantities for river defence work

Box faggots For some customers, size and compactness in the faggots they bought were crucial. Woodmen responded by producing what they called a *box faggot*. You make these in a 1.2m(4ft) frame (fig. 129), cutting all of the sticks to that size, and sandwiching sticks between layers of twigs. To produce a really tight faggot, pass the rope around the sticks and compress them by pushing on the lever and jamming it under the hook whilst you tie the bond.

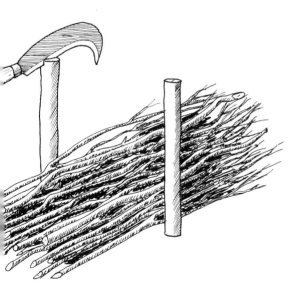

128 To making a faggot use two posts to contain the sticks, making them easier to bind

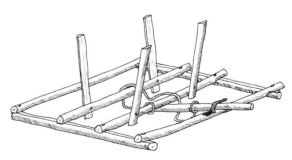

129 Frame for box faggots: stack the sized sticks between the posts, and compress them using the rope and lever. Use the clip to hold the lever down, leaving your two hands free for tying

Bavins and bunce Evelyn was right that too much small wood was unacceptable to many customers. But not so to the poor; for them the smaller wood was made into bundles called *bavins*.

Bunce was bundles of all the smallest wood and rubbish left after the brash had been faggoted. Many older woodmen tell how, as lads working with their fathers, they were allowed to bundle the rubbish and sell it themselves to earn a little pocket money. It truly was their bunce.

FASCINES FOR RIVER WORK

Fascines are still commonly used for coastal and river defence work. They are nothing more than long faggots, being bundles of about 20 small 25mm(1in) rods 2.4–3m(8–10ft) long, bound in three places to give a finished diameter of about 260mm(10in) (fig. 127b). Make them in the same way as you do faggots, but use three pairs of posts to hold them for binding. Nowadays hazel and willow are the preferred material, and must make up 75 per cent of each fascine.

WOOD FUEL

Firewood If you work a hornbeam woodland, you will know from Chapter Two that you have no choice but to sell firewood; nor will you if managing a neglected coppice. But in even the best run wood there will be some material too poor for any craft use yet from which you can make a return as firewood.

In Chapter Six we saw how to set up a cord in which to collect branchwood. Cut any waste wood 1.2m(4ft) long, remove all the knots and branches, and lay each piece in the cord straight; If you don't, when you come to unload it you will have created a lot of hard work for yourself! Cordwood is best left two or even three years to season before being sold as firewood: remember green wood hissing on the fire throws out little heat, and is quite unsuitable for wood stoves. Try to sell as much as you can

in the cord if you do not have a saw bench on which to log it efficiently. There is a strong market in bagged or bulk delivered logs, most people preferring 300mm(1ft) logs split in half. You can log by chainsaw with the help of an assistant if you cannot afford a saw bench.

Charcoal In John Evelyn's day charcoal was the major product of many coppices.* Oak was *charred* for iron works, alder and lime to make gunpowder, and any species to make *small coles* for the hearths of London. As many as 12 cords of wood, stacked on a 7.2m(24ft) diameter hearth and covered with sods to make a kiln, would be charred in one *burn*, which needed four or five days of continuous attention from the *wood colliers* who practised this art. Charcoal is now produced in steel kilns (*see* fig. 172, page 150), mainly to utilize poor wood and to supplement the woodman's other more profitable activities. For those wishing to pursue it further, a small-scale method using oil drums is described in Appendix Four, and the New Woodmanship Trust report (*see* Bibliography) is recommended.

PULPWOOD

Green logs from which to make pulp for the paper and board industry may seem hardly a traditional craft, but since it is an important outlet for coppice wood, any woodland manager ought to be aware of it. Ironically for conservationists the pulp mill at Sittingbourne in Kent has just switched exclusively to re-cycling paper, jeopardizing the future of that county's chestnut woods!

Cut and stack pulpwood as for cordwood, in 1.2m(4ft) lengths, using any poles between 100mm(4in) and 300mm(12in) diameter. Do not cord any dead wood, and deliver it within 12 months of felling.

---

* John Evelyn, *Sylva, or a discourse on forest trees*, (ed. J. Hunter), London, 1786

CHAPTER ELEVEN

BESOM BROOMS

Some years ago one of the few remaining besom makers still using ash bonds to bind his broomheads, displayed his product at a country fair. Young children coming upon the piled besoms and crying almost without exception, 'Oh look – witches' broomsticks!' drew a wry smile from his face. Growing up in an age where malleable man-made plastics have ousted natural materials, they could not know as did children 50 or 100 years ago that besoms were regularly used in many spheres of life.

ABOUT BESOMS OR TWIG BROOMS

A HISTORY OF BESOMS

A besom is defined as 'a bundle of twigs tied round a stick for sweeping' (fig. 130). Pliable twiggy branches have probably been used since pre-history to clean both home and workplace. The best material – long, thin, flexible, resilient yet densely branched – grows only on certain shrubs, and it is ironic that broom, which has an almost perfect structure and was named after the sweeping implement, is no longer used to make besoms since both the bush and the heaths and commons on which it throve are now less frequent. Butchers broom, that short spiky shrub with flattened stems in place of leaves, was used to clean wooden chopping boards. But most broom or besom *heads* were, and still are, made from birch or heather (ling). When fitted with a *tail* (or handle) their springy twigs have a unique ability to lift damp leaves from grass, brush fresh snow from a path, and when worn, to tease moss from a lawn. In use, their balance, weight and slightly irregular

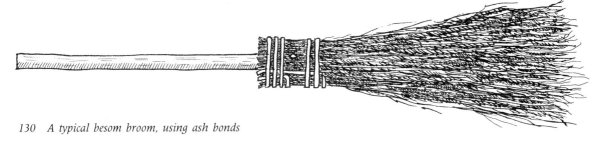

130   A typical besom broom, using ash bonds

handle make for light work, the more so since twigs do not snag like a wire rake. Every cottage, rural workshop, farm, and many factories used besoms regularly until the appearance of alternatives such as the new 'wail bone' broom in the early nineteenth century.

Fine branchwood decays quickly, so nothing remains to us of the earliest besoms. But we can be sure that Iron Age man, who without sophisticated tools could weave and bind hazel rods to make a hut, could also bundle twigs as gypsies do today. It was only the advent of cheap steel wire as an alternative binding that reduced the besomer's entire dependence on the coppice.

Industry found uses for besoms beyond that of simply clearing up: tail-less besoms, known as *swales*, are still used in some ironworks to remove the scale from red hot steel, because in their last moments as they blaze to ash and smoke some unknown alchemy occurs that helps to purify the steel. And birch twigs laid top to tail in even bundles are used in vinegar making to clarify the final liquor (fig. 131).

A better means of clearing leaves and rubbish from the grass of park and golf course has yet to be devised, so a small but steady market for besoms still remains, and with it the skills of the besomer.

DIFFERENT BROOM PATTERNS

Wherever twig brooms are made, even in the United States (see Langsner – bibliography), the basic pattern is similar: a bundle of fine twigs app. 900mm(3ft) long for the head, fitted to a handle app. 1m(3ft 6in) long, giving a finished broom of about 1.5m(5ft). Handle lengths and finished besom sizes were often adjusted to meet a customer's personal preference or local markets, a nicety rarely practised today.

A common variation was in the number of sticks used to make the head. These were roughly gauged into '10 inch' or '12 inch' heads, describing the finished circumference after binding, and the besoms were then sold according to their size. Most commonly besoms

have two *bonds* or *laps* binding the head, though three are sometimes used, and these may be clefts of bramble, ash, hazel, chestnut or oak. No rigid regional pattern emerges in the use of bindings, each woodman's choice being determined by a combination of what is available, what his father taught him and what his own experience has shown him is best.

THE TOOLS AND MATERIALS REQUIRED

TOOLS

The methods described are those used in the coppice rather than those of the village *broom squire* in his workshop. You will need a billhook, side-axe, draw-knife, shave, cleave, auger, knife and bond poker.

The edge tools and their use were described in Chapter Four. The bond or lap poker, however, is a tool unique to besom making. Its purpose is to allow the free end of the bond to be securely tucked away under itself and so produce a binding both tight and secure. Many specialized tools for achieving this have been described, ranging from enormous needles to a hollowed-out gondola shaped metal tool within which the binding can be slipped (fig. 132).

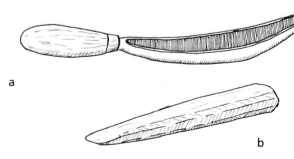

131 (Opposite) *Bundles of birch twigs to be used by vinegar makers to clarify the liquor*

132 (Above) *Bond pokers: (a) a hollowed metal version; (b) a simpler hardwood wedge*

These are rarely seen, and many besomers use a small, polished hardwood wedge to lift the binding a little – it works well and is easy to make.

A BESOMER'S HORSE

You will make much better besoms with a horse: it is essential for shaving the handles or tails, for peeling the ash bonds if you are to use them, and it will allow you to tighten the bonds more effectively than any other method.

A standard horse with a flat plate under the jaws will serve quite satisfactorily for all three jobs, but if you really get to mass production, a modified vice using a forked stick (fig. 133) will grasp the handles better for shaping and smoothing.

THE RIGHT RAW MATERIALS

Every part of a besom comes from the coppice, and the particular requirements for each item are matched by the unique properties of certain trees or shrubs.

Heads Birch makes besom heads *par excellence* (*see* Chapter Two), although you must be careful to select and store it correctly for the best results. Cut or simply wrench the spray or *brish*,

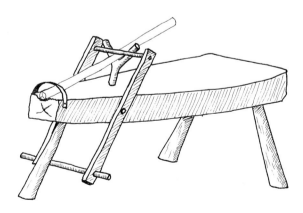

133 A besomer's horse: the forked stick gives a better grip on the round poles used to make handles

none of which should be thicker than 9mm ($\frac{3}{8}$in), from young poles whilst leafless and before the terminal twigs start to droop with age. Since besom making is a spring and summer job, tie the fine twigs into bundles sufficient for about six brooms, and stack them off the ground, alternate bundles reversed butt to head, and each layer at right angles to the one before so that air can flow through the stack. This will also help to flatten the brish before you make the heads, and in this form you can hold it five or six months without it becoming too sere, or too damp and mouldy to be of use.

Heather or ling is also commonly used for heads. Harvest it when it is neither too long, straggly and woody, nor too short as after recent burning. Select bushy stems 600–900mm (2–3ft) long, testing to see if the finer branches are brittle; if they are the broom will be no use, shedding more pieces than it clears; if they are supple, then they are fit to use. Heather should be cut in February or March – certainly before any game birds start nesting, since they are probably more valuable than the heather – and stored in a similar way to birch.

Handles (or tails) Almost any reasonably straight pole of about 40mm($1\frac{1}{2}$in) diameter will provide a handle. Hazel, birch or lime are most often used, but you will find willow and ash poles are every bit as good if you do not have a better use for them. Select suitable poles when you are felling the coppice, and store them bundled and stacked in the shade, where they will remain workable for six or seven months.

Bindings Usable bonds, 1.2m(4ft) long, thin, and flexible enough to bind the head, can be obtained in several ways, each requiring different material. Firstly withes can be used: for these select very small 6mm($\frac{1}{4}$in) rods of hazel or willow which can be cut from one-or two-year-old growth in the coppice.

Larger, knot-free rods (about 25mm(1in) diameter) of ash, hazel, oak and chestnut can be riven down to make flat splits for use as bonds. As you select suitable rods when cutting the coppice, you may find them very tender when first cut from the stool, making it difficult to produce the fine clefts required, so it is best to let them dry for a few weeks before use.

Bramble is still used by some besomers. Those long, grasping, arched shoots that have grown vigorously for one year make the best bonds. To grow 1.2m(4ft) in one year is nothing special for a vigorous blackberry plant, and one craftsman claims to have cut a 4.8m(16ft) stem from which to make his bonds!!* Unlike other material, you can cut bramble and use it immediately, at which stage it makes the best of all bonds; but like the others it deteriorates with keeping, its supple strength drying into sapless inflexibility after three or four weeks.

MAKING A BESOM BROOM

In most coppices, besom-making is rarely a full-time job; it is one part of the woodman's work, to be fitted in when more demanding jobs are over and using up material that would otherwise be wasted. Nevertheless brooms should be produced efficiently, and working a full day a good man can make three dozen.

BONDS OR LAPS TO BIND THE HEAD

Withe That most ancient and original woodland binding, the withe (*see* Chapter Ten), is the simplest. Take the 6mm($\frac{1}{4}$in) rods of hazel, birch or willow you have put aside, and trim the smaller end obliquely to give a long point that can be inserted easily between the sticks when binding them. Then simply wind the rod as you would a withe to produce a bond ready for immediate use; and if it unwinds a little before use, then just give it another couple of twists.

Ash Fine clefts of ash (called ash-splits in the USA), 12mm($\frac{1}{2}$in) wide and creamy white, look so well against the dark birch twigs which they hold tightly without biting or breaking, that many besomers rate them the best binding. Although these clefts are only 1.5mm($\frac{1}{16}$in) thick, they are immensely tough, displaying the exceptional strength of wood-fibres along the grain.

To make them cut 1.2m(4ft) lengths from rods about 30mm($1\frac{1}{4}$in) in diameter, and using a large holly or box wood cleave, rive them into three clefts as described in Chapter Seven. Now sit astride the horse with a good hessian sack or similar protecting your right leg, and remove the pith and core wood by drawing each triangualr cleft back under your knife blade, to leave a thick flat cleft. Insert the knife at one end of this piece, carefully lift a 1.5mm($\frac{1}{16}$in) thick cleft, and by twisting the

134   Peeling a cleft from an ash rod to make a bond. The cleft is peeled back with the right hand, whilst the left hand controls the thickness

---

* John Stannard, *Norfolk Craftsmen*, Boydell Press, 1979

knife backwards and forwards extend it at least 100mm(4in) along the stuff. Now place the lower (and thicker) cleft in the jaws of the horse, grasp it tightly, and then carefully peel back the finer cleft (fig. 134). As the clefts become longer you will have to feed the bottom one intermittently through the jaws of the horse, and re-clamp it. The skill lies in maintaining an even thickness, which is achieved by controlling the curve, and therefore tension applied to the lower cleft, at the point of splitting. Holding the wood straight will make the top cleft thin and eventually run out; bending it more will make the upper cleft thicker as the split moves towards the fibres under tension. Keep peeling until you have a full 1.2m(4ft) long bond, which you must then clean of spears and thin down at any thick spots by carefully drawing it under your knife (fig. 135). Finally point one end bluntly, and your bond is ready for use. Use it without delay, because these very fine clefts soon dry and loose their suppleness.

Similarly fine clefts of hazel can be obtained by peeling them from round rods. Using a knife, slice obliquely into the side of a rod and lift a 1.5mm($\frac{1}{16}$in) thick flap. Continue to peel this cleft along the rod as shown in figure 136, bending the rod to thicken the cleft, or straightening it to thin it.

Bramble Most woodmen view bramble as a bind, not a binding, and the American name of 'blasphemy vine' is very apt! But to the besomer it is a source of bonds *par excellence*.

Select a straight 1.2m(4ft) length and *shrie* it of its prickles either by pulling it through a very thickly gloved hand or by using a knife. Be very careful to avoid cutting the outer woody fibres which give the bramble its toughness. Split the stem into two by inserting your knife into one end and twisting it to lever the stem apart as you would if riving a rod with a billhook.

Complete the two bonds by removing the central pith from each one by holding the knife firmly against it and pulling the cleft backwards under the knife which will cause the pith to curl up and out.

PICKING AND BINDING THE HEAD

Pick the sticks required for the head from the bundles you cut in the coppice, putting to one side any that are sere. To gauge whether you have sufficient, place your two hands around the bunched stems: if your index fingers and thumbs just meet around the bundle there is sufficient for a '12 inch' head, whereas if they overlap to their first joint you have enough for a '10 inch' head. These sizes refer to the finished

135 Remove thick spots from a cleft by pulling it under a knife

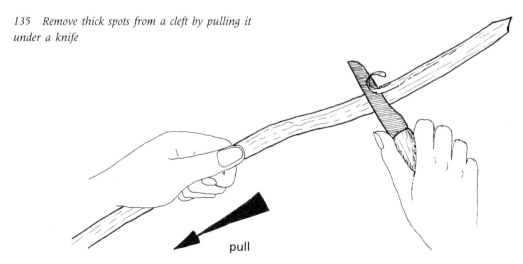

pull

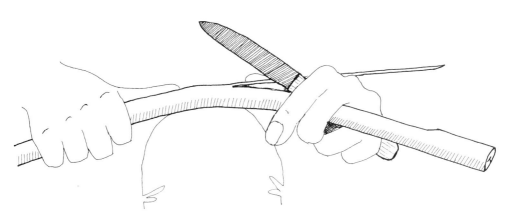

136 Peeling a cleft from a hazel rod using a knife: the rod is bent over the knee to control the thickness of the cleft

circumference of the head and allow for the compression imposed by tight bonds.

If most of the sticks are of similar length, just bang them butts-down a couple of times to get them roughly level and make sure the outer ones are carefully placed to give a smooth head; if your sticks vary in length put the longer ones in the centre with shorter bushier ones around them to create a slightly tapered head.

To understand how to bind a head, read this description in conjunction with fig. 138. Sit on your horse with one end of the bond held tightly in the vice jaws. Bring the other end over and round the head, inserting it between the sticks about 150mm(6in) from their butts. Now gripping the head in both hands, pull hard against the clamped vice to tighten the bond, and keeping it under tension, roll the head to wind more of the bond round it (fig. 137), until it is encircled by three tight laps. To tie off the bond, hold it tightly to prevent it loosening, insert your bond poker under it to make a sufficient tunnel for the free end to be poked through, and finally twist the bond, push it underneath the laps, and pull it out the far side until it is tight.

Apply a second bond in the same way as the first, this time starting 50mm(2in) from the butt end, giving it three or four loops which pass over the free end of the previous bond, and finish with a free end parallel and about 25mm(1in) away from its predecessor.

The bound head is finished by squaring up its butt end to give a clean, level surface. Do this on a chopping block using a heavy bill-hook or better still a side-axe, leaving about 25mm(1in) of stick protruding beyond the last bond; you will get a cleaner cut by rolling the head a little as you chop it.

SMOOTHING THE TAIL

Cut your tail or handle poles to 0.9m(3ft) on a sawing horse and point them with a side-axe. If you are going to leave the bark on, sharpen to a point 150mm(6in) long with a small square at the tip and remove any buds flush, leaving the tail ready for use.

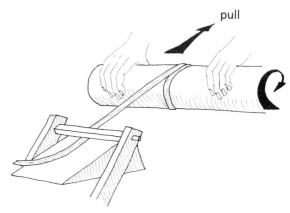

137 Use the vice on a horse to help tighten the bond; pull and twist at the same time

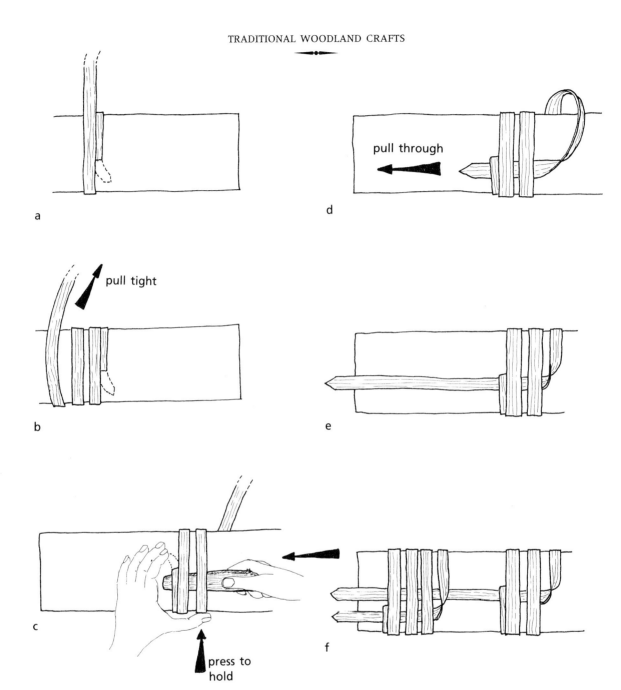

138 Binding a besom. (a) to (e) show how to tie a
bond; the second bond (f) requires the same method

The best besoms have a rinded and
smoothed tail. To produce these, hold the pole
in a horse (fig. 133) after sharpening, and using your draw-knife remove the bark and buds,
and lengthen the point a little more. Since the

draw-knife will leave a series of flat surfaces
on a round pole, you will need a small curved
shave (fig. 46b) to achieve a smooth round
handle. Use it in a similar fashion to the draw-
knife (fig. 139), removing fine shavings and
rotating the tail as necessary. Sometimes around
knots you will find the shave pulls up some
wood fibres leaving a rough patch, and you
can remove these by shaving in the opposite

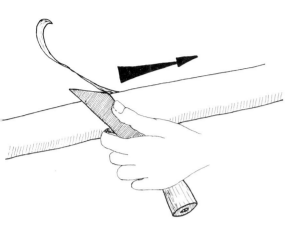

139 *Use a curved shave to smooth the handle. Note the way it is held*

direction, leaving the handle smooth and comfortable to use, but with just enough irregularity to grip in a wet hand.

FINISHING OFF

Head and tail must now be mated to complete the besom. Force the sharpened point of the tail into the bound end of the head as near to the centre as possible, and then grasping the tail firmly bang it down on the chopping block. At each blow you will see the head slide a little further down the tail, carried by its own momentum, and compressing the twigs even more tightly within the grip of the bonds. Gauge how far the tail has penetrated the head by standing another beside it on the block, and stop when you see that the end is an inch or two beyond the second binding (fig. 140). If the tail does not enter straight you can usually lever it back (fig. 141); rarely you will have to remove it and start again.

It is usual to peg the head and tail together. Make the pegs or *spicks* from the triangular clefts of ash or hazel used to prepare the bindings. Sharpen one end of the cleft with three strokes of either knife or hook, then chop the sharpened end off to make a peg 100mm(4in) long. In order to fit this right through both head and tail, hold the besom under your knee and use an auger to drill a 9mm($\frac{3}{8}$in) hole right through head and tail between the two bonds. Then drive the spick home through this hole using the poll of your axe. Finally, should any surplus peg protrude, cut it off with your knife. When you are really proficient, and after two or three hours have completed a dozen, lay six brooms one way, six the other head to tail, tie all 12 together with two bonds, and stack them beside the ride to await collection.

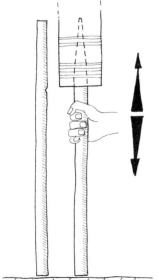
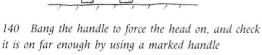

140 *Bang the handle to force the head on, and check it is on far enough by using a marked handle*

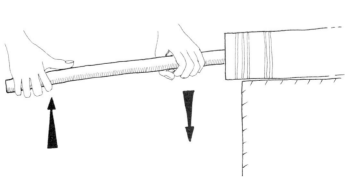

141 *An off-centre handle can often be corrected by simply levering it as shown*

CHAPTER · TWELVE

GATE HURDLES

IN Kingston churchyard, Kent, stands a
gravestone bearing a simple inscription: Jesse
Carl Mummery – Hurdlemaker – died 1955 aged
74. Jesse was one of the best hurdle makers in
East Kent, and the story is told of how at a
farm sale his hurdles were purchased under
cover by the auctioneer, himself a discerning
farmer. Those men demanded much from the
five-bar gate hurdles with which they penned
their sheep: durability and strength, but with a
minimum of weight so a man could move them
easily; and a finish kind to the animals they
restrained. They knew good from mediocre.

This is how Jesse and his contemporaries in
Suffolk made their hurdles:

ABOUT GATE HURDLES

THEIR HISTORY IN ENGLAND

There can be few countrymen who have not at
some time used a gate hurdle (fig. 142). Used
primarily for penning or *folding* sheep, they
made a major contribution to the agricultural
changes of the seventeenth and eighteenth
centuries. When, in the 1730s, Viscount 'Turnip' Townshend made East Anglian farming

pre-eminent with his Norfolk four-course rotation, it was ash gate hurdles that allowed sheep
to be folded on the turnip crop that was one of
these rotations, providing for the first time
winter feed for animals and fresh meat all year.
Folding was also used to control the grazing
and manuring of the grass downlands and
coastal marshes so famous for their sheep. Folds
were also an inseparable part of spring lambing and summer sheep sales where wooden
hurdles contained each farmer's lot. In addition stout hurdles were used by almost every
cottager to pen his pig, whilst yet more massive ones contained young bullocks at the sales.

Hurdles had a hard life. Although holes
for the feet were started by the shepherd's
metal *fold-pitch* or *peeler*, heavy blows were
needed to erect them in the frost-hard ground
of winter; and two days later they were shaken
loose, humped on the shepherd's back, and
the process repeated. Mixed farming, blending
animals and arable, provided a large market
for these tough, durable hurdles. But the
relentless changes in agriculture, particularly
the increased arable acreage occasioned by the
Second World War, and light-weight electric
fencing, all gradually reduced demand, and
rendered hurdlemaking virtually a thing of the

122

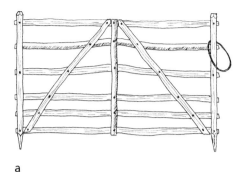

a

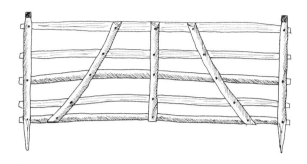

b

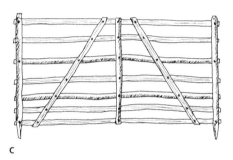

c

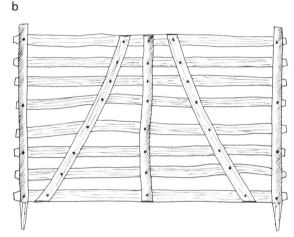

d

142 Different patterns of hurdles:
a   Suffolk – note metal loop for fixing to a shore
b   Kent – note ferrules and long foot
c   Hampshire
d   A massive bullock hurdle

past. A handful of traditional hurdlemakers remain in Kent and Suffolk making their product for the discerning few, in competition with the makers of heavy 'gates' in rip-sawn wood whose weight matters little to men who carry nothing unless it's on a tractor.

DIFFERENT REGIONAL PATTERNS

Gate hurdle patterns vary from county to county, and occasionally with the passage of time: for example pre-1900 photographs show Suffolk-made hurdles that differ markedly from those produced in the county during the last 50 years. Most variations occur in the number of *rails* (*slays* in Kent or *ledges* in Suffolk) used, and the positioning of the *braces* (fig. 142).

An East Anglian gate is 1.8m(6ft) long by 1.2m(4ft) high with six ledges morticed into a *head* at either end. A *foot* of only 150mm(6in) is left below the bottom ledge, since although the hurdles may be driven into the ground, for the most part they are supported by posts (*shores*), and to allow this a metal loop may be fitted between the top two ledges of each hurdle during manufacture. Each brace usually reaches all the way from the vertical *strop* to the heads at either end. This pattern is also typical in Essex and Sussex, but in Hampshire and Wiltshire, where gates are often called *flakes*, seven ledges are used and the braces do not normally meet the heads.

Kentish hurdles are quite different: 2.4m (8ft) long by 1.2m(4ft) high with only five ledges and a large 375mm(15in) foot which is sufficient, when driven into the ground, to support the hurdle. Such heavy use demands a ferrule at the top of the head to prevent it splitting.

One feature common to all gates is having a smaller gap between the bottom three ledges than the remainder. This closer spacing prevents the older sheep putting their heads through the fold, since, like men, they always believe the grass is greener on the other side; and if it is, the shepherd wants the lambs to have it!

A pig hurdle needed to be stronger, and although the same size as those for sheep, always contained seven ledges made from stouter clefts; and a bullock hurdle was 1.8m(6ft) high with eight ledges and a much heavier construction (fig. 142d).

Tools and Materials Required

THE TOOLS AND DEVICES

Wherever gate hurdles are made, the tools used are very similar: you will need a saw for cutting poles to length; a froe for riving them; a draw-knife for rinding and shaping; a side-axe for sharpening; a brace to drill mortices; and finally a chisel or *morticing knife* to cut and finish the mortices. Tool patterns and use were covered in detail in chapter four except the morticing knife. This tool, also called a *twybil* (fig. 143c), is peculiar to gate-hurdle making amongst the coppice crafts, being most commonly used in the southern counties of England; other craftsmen it seems still prefer a chisel and mallet. Derived from the much larger carpenter's moticing tools of the late Middle Ages, the word twybil is probably a corruption of 'two-bill' which described the two functions of the tool: first to cut the sides of the mortice; and secondly to lever out the waste wood. Its used is described later, but suffice to say it is unquestionably the best tool for morticing green wood. Unfortunately they are extremely difficult to obtain, and you will probably have to take the dimensions given in Appendix One and have one made.

No woodman can work fast or accurately, however good his tools, without suitable devices to hold his material in exactly the right position. These 'horses', 'brakes' and 'stools' were discussed in Chapter Five, and are crucially important in making gate hurdles. You need to choose from those described, a sawing horse, a riving brake, a shaving horse, and finally a morticing stool or horse.

THE RIGHT RAW MATERIAL

Hurdles are made from various woods, local differences being dictated mainly by that which is available. In southern England willow is favoured, being light and easy to work fresh cut from the stool, even though it rots more quickly. In the mixed woodlands of East Anglia woodmen prefer ash, but will use hazel, elm and even oak where they naturally arise. In Kent chestnut is used and it is unquestionably the best, for both heads and bottom rails (where a hurdle rots first) last twice as long if made of it. Whichever wood you do use, you must get clean, straight poles to make good hurdles.

Making a Gate Hurdle

HEADS AND LEDGES

Select good, straight 75mm(3in) diameter poles for your heads; those for ledges can be from 50mm(2in) and slightly bowed. Smooth off any knots with a side-axe. Using a notched measuring stick (fig. 143a) mark out the best quality lengths from the poles you have, and cut them to size using a bow-saw. Cut the heads to their true length, but the ledges approximately 38mm(1½in) longer than the width of the hurdle you are to make, allowing them to protrude a little through the heads. Thus to make an East Anglian hurdle you should cut one at 1.2m(4ft) for the heads, three at 1.84m(6ft 1½in) for the ledges, one at 1.05m(3ft

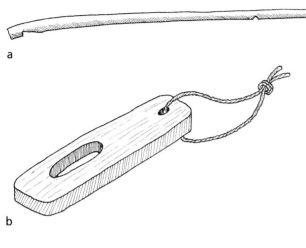

a

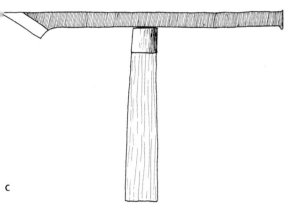

b

c

143   Special tools of the hurdlemaker:
a   Notched measuring rod
b   Gauge for ends of ledges
c   Twybil or morticing knife

6in) for the strop and one at 1.5m(5ft) for the braces.

Now rive the poles, using your froe or doll-axe, beetle and riving brake, whose use has already been described in Chapter Seven. Carefully rive the two heads from the one pole so they are mirror clefts with similar curves. Likewise rive any poles up to 75mm(3in) diameter once to give two ledges or braces. Larger ones you will have to split into more clefts: for example a 130mm(5in) pole should give six ledges.

Ledges   Take the long clefts intended for ledges to your rinding dog or brake, and using a draw-knife firstly smooth the face and chamfer the edges of each cleft, removing any spears that could injure stock penned by the finished hurdle. Now remove all the bark. Leave the smallest clefts round backed, but to lighten the hurdle shave larger ones to leave them 25mm(1in) thick (fig. 144), and you should do this as you rind them. Any quarter clefts resulting from larger poles should also be shaped to produce a flat ledge (fig. 144b), using your draw-knife, or side-axe if you prefer. Any clefts that exhibit a *wind*, and some will, you must carefully shave on opposite sides at each end in order to produce a ledge as flat as possible otherwise they may twist the finished hurdle out of shape.

Finally, whilst each ledge is still in the brake both ends must be shaped or *tipped*. Aim to produce an end tapering gently to about 19mm($\frac{3}{4}$in) thick by 44mm($1\frac{3}{4}$in) long (fig. 144d). This is best done using a draw-knife, giving a neat flattened oval shape, as shown, to fit the mortices. It is a good idea to use a gauge (fig. 143b), which you can slip over the end of the ledge to confirm your sizing is correct.

Heads   Clean and rind the two clefts to be used as heads in the same way as the ledges. Then, taking your side-axe, sharpen the bottom of the head to produce a pointed foot; leave a small 9mm($\frac{3}{8}$in) square at the tip, and give a 150mm(6in) taper to the foot. You should also use your axe to champfer the top in order to reduce its tendency to split when hit if driving it into the ground. This problem is more severe with longer footed Kentish hurdles designed to be self-supporting, and the answer to this problem is to fit a ferrule around the top of the

125

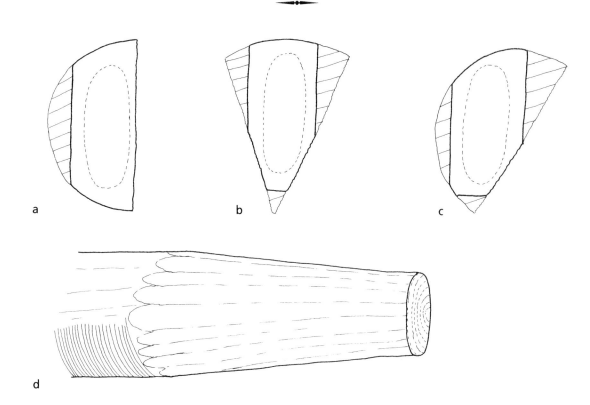

144 *Shaping ledges: in (a) to (c) the hatched areas show the waste wood you should remove; (c) shows how to straighten a wound cleft; and (d) how the end of each ledge should be tipped*

head (fig. 145). These are made from 1.5mm ($\frac{1}{16}$in) × 25mm(1in) mild steel strip. Sometimes these were made by the hurdlemaker himself, cutting the strip to 175mm(7in) lengths on a guillotine, punching out the three holes, over-lapping the free ends and finally rivetting them together. Today it is simpler to purchase fer-rules from a blacksmith, who will normally weld them in preference to rivetting. Champfer the inside edge of the ferrule at one end with a file so that it will go over the head more easily.

Offer the ferrule to the end of the head whilst it is still in the shaving dog, and tap it with your hammer to leave an imprint of its shape. Then carefully shave the head down to this mark. Do not shave it too small or the head will still be able to split within the ferrule when it is hit. Once the size is right, knock the ferrule on, hitting it alternately at either end so it goes on straight, and when it is flush with the top of the head, fix it with a 19mm($\frac{3}{4}$in) nail.

MARKING UP

The real skill in hurdlemaking is to utilize variable material yet produce a strong, flat hurdle with a minimum of waste. This is how it is done. Place an old hurdle on the ground as the *pattern* – it is best to use the same one all the time. Lay the two heads, riven side up, exactly over those of the pattern, followed by the ledges. Selection of these is critical: care-fully choose your top ledge by sighting along it to ensure its top edge will meet flush with the strop (a gap here makes buyers think the hurdle is weak) and if necessary shave it to close up any gap; put the strongest at the top and bottom; and put the weakest – those that may

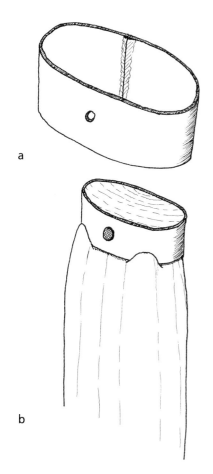

a

b

have run out a little during riving or bear large knots – second and third up from the bottom where they will derive most support from the braces. Unless they are very straight, the two clefts arising from a single pole should be placed one with its riven side down, the other with its riven side up so that any curves in them match, and produce a constant animal-proof gap. Finally, try to oppose any wound clefts in alternate ledges to neutralize their twisting pressure, which will *throw* the finished hurdle.

Whilst they are resting on the heads, mark the length of each mortice by running a pencil along either side of every ledge (fig 146a). Any ledges curved where they meet the head will require a mortice cut at an angle from the true horizontal, and you should note these when you come to cut their mortices. Likewise if you have a very badly wound ledge whose tips you could not straighten sufficiently by shaving, you can mark the mortice to be cut out of the vertical so your hurdle is not thrown.

145 (Above) *Ferrules: (a) a welded mild steel ferrule; (b) the ferrule nailed in place on the top of the head*

146 (Below) *Marking the heads: first draw a pencil line marking the width of the ledge (a); then mark the centres for the holes before drilling to ensure the mortice will be central to the sides of the head (b)*

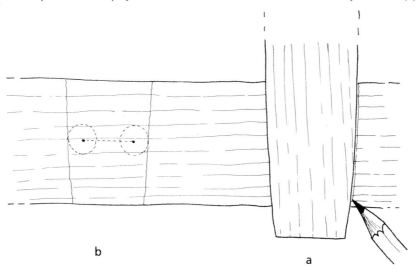

b

a

CUTTING THE MORTICES

A green wood vice (fig. 147) is sometimes used to hold the heads on edge whilst drilling the holes horizontally. The low morticing brake shown in fig. 65 is better, because it allows vertical drilling and completion of the mortice in one position. Using a brace fitted with a 14mm($\frac{9}{16}$ in) twist bit, first mark the centre for every hole (fig. 146b). Once you are satisfied these follow the centre line of the head drill one hole at either end of each mortice, whose outer edge just touches the pencil line you marked on the head. Remember to angle any holes slightly where you have marked that this should be done. Some hurdlemakers used to weight their brace with a cast iron wheel (fig. 148) to improve the performance of the old *shell bits* they used – its sound caused it to be the known as *the growler*! Complete all drilling and subsequent morticing from that side of the head you marked up; this will be the inner facing surface on the finished hurdle, and working from this side will ensure a good fit when mated to the ledges.

148 Drilling a hurdle head using a weighted brace to make the job easier. Note the twybil lying beside the brake

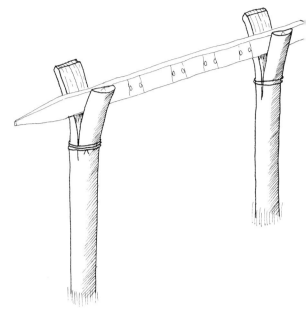

147 A green wood vice which can be used to hold the heads for drilling

Chisel and mallet are the simplest means of finishing the mortices. Sitting astride a small *stool*, simply cut down with a chisel to remove that waste wood remaining between the holes you have drilled. Make sure that the sides of the mortice are smooth, that they taper slightly to fit the ledge, and that you make each mortice wide enough lest the ledge split the head apart when it is driven home.

The twybil A better method of cutting the mortices after drilling is to use a twybil or morticing knife: once mastered it does a faster, neater job, and is used in the brake used for drilling the holes. The following description should be read in conjunction with fig. 149. To remove the slug of waste wood between the holes, first cut up each side of it by inserting the twybil blade at one side of the hole nearest you, as shown. Push down hard, forcing the blade along the grain, and complete the cut to the second hole by levering the tool back towards yourself, pushing down hard on its back stem (fig. 150a). Repeat this on the other side

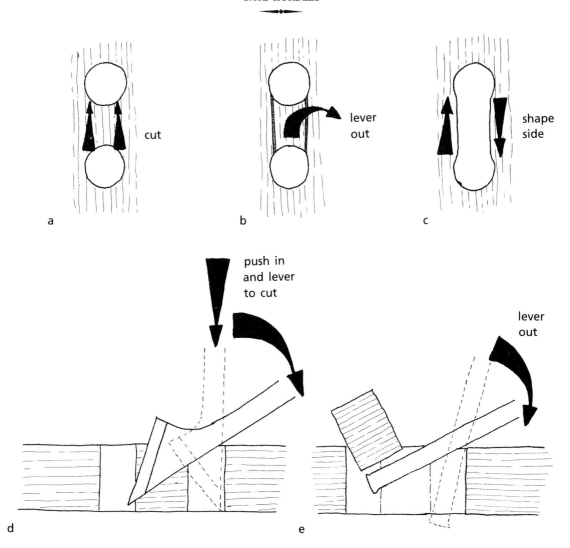

149 *Using the twybil (1): firstly cut along either side of the waste wood (a) and (d); then huck out the waste slug (b) and (e); and finally clean the surplus wood from the sides of mortice (c)*

of the mortice, then turn the twybil over, insert the back stem into the nearer hole, and by pulling back towards you on the handle, *huck* out the waste wood.

Now use the twybil to smooth the sides of the mortice and give it the necessary taper. To do this, hold the tool as shown (fig. 150b): work the blade, starting with the tip but finishing with its whole cutting edge, by

pumping up and down on the handle. Keep the blade moving across the wood to remove shavings; remember, as the name morticing knife suggests, it is designed to cut more like a knife than a chisel.

MAKING UP THE HURDLE

Leave your selected ledges on the pattern and return the heads after morticing so the hurdle can be made up. To one side of the pattern hurdle you should have two short posts protruding 150mm(6in) above the ground (fig. 151). Mate the ledges to the marked side of the head at this end first; then fit the opposing

a

b

150　A twybil should be held as shown in (a) to cut along between the two holes; and as shown in (b) to shape the sides of the mortice

head, remembering the iron hoop if needed, and settle the ledges home into their mortices by holding the hurdle at an angle, and pushing or hammering against the two short posts. Your ledges should project 19mm($\frac{3}{4}$in) beyond the head, hence the reason for cutting them 38mm ($1\frac{1}{2}$in) longer than the hurdle size. If you have

properly gauged, marked and cut both ledges and heads, the whole should fit together firmly but without needing too much force. Once the heads are squared up, lay the vertical strop and two diagonal braces that have been previously cut, rinded and smoothed on top of the hurdle. Cut them 150mm(6in) longer than required so they can be trimmed after nailing.

Nailing-up is best accomplished with the hurdle flat on the ground, after removal from the pattern (fig. 152). Nail only the first, third and last ledges to the heads, but you must nail the braces and strop to every ledge. Never nail braces to the heads. Use 65mm($2\frac{1}{2}$in) nails. Cut rose-head nails are best since they cut through the wood and grip it tightly, but wire nails are adequate. To avoid the ends of the ledges and braces splitting, drill 3mm($\frac{1}{8}$in) holes before nailing. If you can get a blacksmith to fit a 450mm(18in) extension to your twist bit, it will allow relatively comfortable drilling of the hurdle on the floor with your feet holding the components in position. Chestnut and willow take wire nails without pre-drilled holes except at the ends of the braces; ash is best with every nail hole drilled. Clench over the protruding nail ends, about 25mm(1in) to hold the hurdle tight (fig. 151a), ensuring that the tips of the nails have been bent over before clenching so their points are driven back into the wood, thus avoiding injury to animals or to the shepherds' hands.

Woodmen occasionally held the heads on the hurdle by driving small wooden pegs through the morticed ends of the ledges (fig. 151b), the strop and braces still being nailed to each ledge. This did more to impress judges at county shows than it did for the strength or function of the hurdle.

A hurdle should be properly finished. Start by cutting the surplus length of both strops and braces back to the ledges. Then take your draw-knife and champfer the top edge of strop and braces smooth and flush to the top edge. Finally, remove any ragged pieces or splinters. Making your first hurdle will take several hours; when you can make a good one in an hour and a half, you will have mastered the craft.

Store your hurdles by laying them flat on poles that keep them off the ground. Stack them flat on top of one another up to a height of 1.8m(6ft) or more, and if your stack is still horizontal at the top there can be little wrong with your hurdles. Place any with a *kick* (twist) at the bottom where they will be flattened out. Stacked this way the air can pass through them freely, drying and seasoning them quickly.

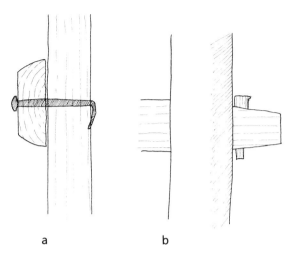

a   b

151   *Clench the ends of the nails over as shown in (a); small wooden pegs can be used to hold the ledges instead of nails (b)*

152   *Nailing up a hurdle in front of the two short posts against which to brace it when tightening the heads on the ledges*

CHAPTER · THIRTEEN

WATTLE HURDLES

'THIRTY years ago there seemed no hope of another generation of hurdlemakers, as the destruction of our coppices was reaching such proportions that one could see no future in it; but today the trend is to go back to the coppice'. Those words, written in 1988 by a Dorset hurdle maker were prophetic: if you order a hurdle today you will be lucky to receive it two years hence!

Making wattles is one of the supreme crafts of woodmanship. It requires no little skill to make resilient, woven fencing panels from small rods, without nails and using only a billhook and your hands. Not only must you learn the craft, you must first master all the basic skills – cutting, trimming, riving and winding a withe. But once you have made your first hurdle you will know real satisfaction, and want to go on making them.

FROM SHEEP FOLDS TO GARDEN SCREENS

A SHORT HISTORY

Wattles of woven hazel and willow are as old as woodmanship: primitive woven hurdles have been recovered from the Somerset Levels where they were laid down by our Neolithic ancestors to provide a trackway across the mire; and we have already seen how Iron Age huts had walls of woven hazel. By the Middle Ages wattle fencing was common, frequently being illustrated in manuscripts and paintings.

It was managing the millions of sheep upon which England's early wealth was built, that gave rise to the classic wattle hurdle. Made as a portable fencing panel light enough for a man to shoulder four at a time, it was perfect for folding sheep to control them when grazing, being dipped, or being sheared. And their great advantage over gate hurdles is that at lambing time they offer more protection from wind and rain.

Although today wattle hurdles are largely replaced by lambing sheds and electric fencing, a strong demand for screens or fencing panels has taken their place. Made in a variety of sizes, these panels look well in gardens, and can be made in-situ as continuous fencing.

DIFFERENT PATTERNS OF HURDLE

A basic sheep hurdle is 1.8m(6ft) long by 1m($3\frac{1}{2}$ ft) high woven around ten *uprights* or *zales* (fig. 153) to give a tight weave. At either end the last two zales are longer so that adjacent hurdles can be overlapped and fixed to a post or *shore* using a twisted hazel *shackle*. A gap (the *twilley* hole) is left in the weave between the centre two zales, through which the shepherd passes a stick in order to carry the hurdle on his back, and ten sharpened feet project at the bottom to grip soft ground.

These are the key features of a woven sheep hurdle, but you will find regional differences in the patterns of weaving (fig. 153). In Dorset, for example, round rods at the base of the weave are finished off to a straight line, whilst the twilley hole extends to one side; Hampshire hurdlemakers leave their base rods uneven, saying the sloping weave helps to shed water; and those in Sussex insert their rods into the weave quite differently, giving a distinctive pattern. A less common pattern was the *lamb creep*: this had three large holes in the centre through which lambs could squeeze to have first bite at the new grass. To strengthen sheep hurdles, which were constantly being moved from place to place, the *bottom binders* were taken twice round each end zale, and to make the shepherd's life a little easier, no rods projected at the back of the hurdle to snag his clothes.

Garden screens, today's major market for woven hurdles, were developed from the sheep hurdle. From 910mm(3ft) to 1.8m(6ft) high, they have only nine zales, the least you can have to make a tight weave, and no twilley hole.

153   *Hurdle patterns: (a) Dorset sheep hurdle; (b) Sussex sheep hurdle; (c) lamb creep hurdle; (d) garden screen, Hampshire weave. The method of picking up both bottom and top rods is the same for all types, but the pattern of the middle binders differs*

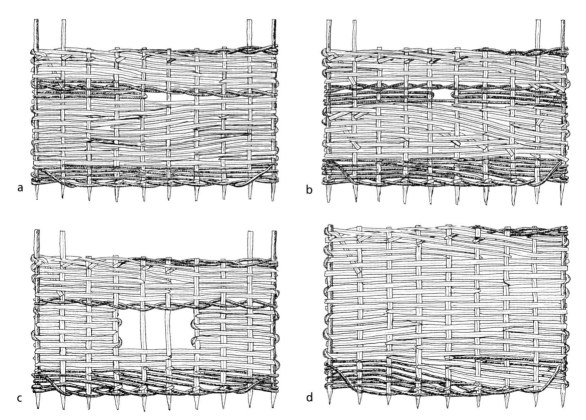

a

b

c

d

TOOLS AND MATERIALS REQUIRED

THE TOOLS AND DEVICES

Although essentially simple, a hurdlemaker's tools are distinctive and highly effective. To trim and rive long hazel rods you will need a hurdlemaker's long-nosed billhook (fig. 30), and to trim the finished hurdle either a *hurdle hook* (fig. 154a) or a *nug* (or *noggin*) axe (fig. 154b). These last two are very difficult to obtain these days, so you may have to do with the shortest nosed hook you can find. You may also rive your rods with an adze (*see* Chapter Seven).

The remaining devices needed to set up your hurdling *pitch* you can make yourself, and are shown in fig. 156. Of these the most important

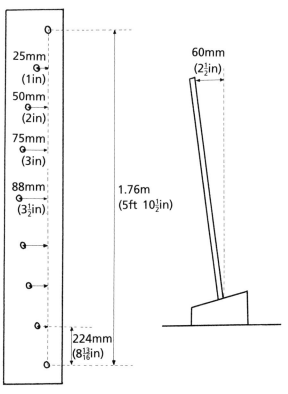

155   Hurdle mould or frame: for a ten zale hurdle make the holes 200mm(7 $\frac{13}{16}$ in) apart, with an extra 1.5mm($\frac{1}{16}$ in) in the three centre gaps

25mm (1in)
50mm (2in)
75mm (3in)
88mm (3$\frac{1}{2}$in)

1.76m (5ft 10$\frac{1}{2}$in)

60mm (2$\frac{1}{2}$in)

224mm (8$\frac{13}{16}$in)

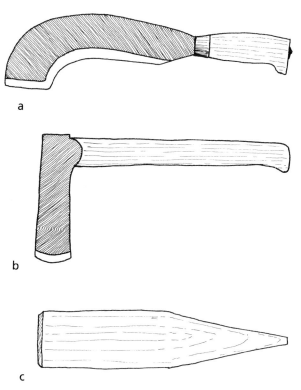

154   Hurdlemaker's tools: (a) a handbill for trimming the completed hurdle; (b) a nug-axe for the same purpose, with a blade only 38mm(1$\frac{1}{2}$in) wide; (c) a beetle or mallet, squared from an ash butt, for knocking down the weavers

is the hurdle *mould* or *frame*. Ideally for this you require a 2.1m(7ft) long curved log of at least 150mm(6in) diameter which you split centrally. If you cannot find a curved log, use a beam at least 75mm(3in) thick and 180mm(7in) wide to accommodate the curved line of holes required for the zales. To set out the holes, first mark the end two at a distance of 1.76m (5ft 10in): this will produce a 1.8m(6ft) hurdle when the rods are wound around the end zales. Tap in a nail at these two points, then join them with a length of string. Using this straight line together with the set-backs and spacings for nine or ten zale hurdles shown in fig. 155, mark the positions for the remaining holes. Drill 16mm($\frac{5}{8}$in) diameter holes right through the mould at a slight backward angle so that each

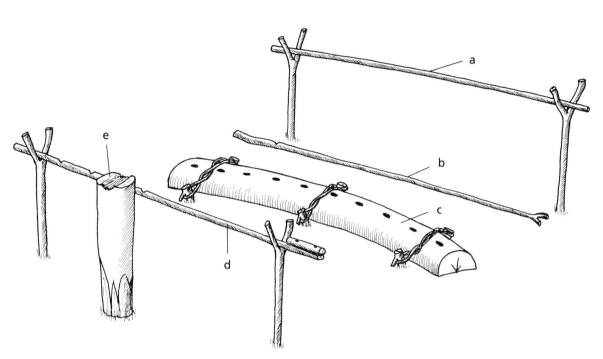

156 Hurdlemaker's pitch: the devices are, from the back: rod horse (a); hurdle gauge stick (b); mould or frame (c); zale gauge (d); chopping block (e). Note the hazel bonds and pegs which hold the mould

zale's top will be 63mm(2½in) back from the base. Curved hurdles are said to tighten up when stacked flat, whilst angled zales makes both inserting and compressing the weaving rods easier.

Use three bonds, each held by two pegs cut from forked branches (fig. 156), to steady the mould.

For a chopping block use a stout post, and for the *rod horse* or *gallows*, two progs and a long stick. Your *hurdle gauge stick* should be straight, with a crotch at one end, a notch to mark the 1.8m(6ft) point, and a further 150mm(6in) with which to hold it. Make your *zale gauge stick* by nailing a block to one end of a straight stick and notching the other end to denote the zale heights required – normally at 1.33m(4ft 5in), 1.63m(5ft 5in) and 1.93m(6ft 5in). The extra 130mm(5in) allows for the *foot* which extends beyond the bottom of the weave. Finally make

yourself a flat sided *mallet* or beetle (fig. 154c) from a round pole, using your side-axe. You are now ready to start wattling!

THE BEST MATERIALS

As we saw in Chapter Two, English wattle hurdles are made of hazel wood. But do not overlook willow: it rives and winds as well as hazel, and although it does not last quite as long, it has been used for centuries in Europe.

MAKING A WATTLE HURDLE

The descriptions which follow outline how a wattle screen of nine zales is made. Any differences from the traditional ten zale sheep hurdle are highlighted.

Firstly sort the rods roughly by length and quality, zales and finishing rods requiring the best. Use straight rods about 31mm(1¼in) diameter for the zales, cleaning off any knots smoothly. Leave the end zales round, but rive the remainder carefully so that each split is central, for any thin points will allow them to be bent by the weavers. After sharpening the zales to a 130mm(5in) long, clean straight point that is neither curved nor feather pointed (fig. 157), put each one into the zale gauge, and use a billhook to mark the rod at the appropriate length for the size of hurdle you are making; then, zale on block, cut it squarely to length.

The zales can now be fitted into the frame. If the round ones for each end are slightly bent, straighten them before fitting them into their holes. Most split zales will have a slight curve, which arises when riving releases the tensions in the round rod. Whatever the cause, you must fit these zales to the frame so that any curves all face the same way (fig. 158). Use your mallet to knock them in so they are level, with their entire point in the frame. The end zales need to be firm, but remember they do have to come out again!

PICKING UP THE BOTTOM OF THE HURDLE

Picking up the initial weave (fig. 159) properly is crucial; without it the bottom will, quite literally, fall out of your hurdle. Use round rods of about 19mm($\frac{3}{4}$in) for this because they wind and twist better than clefts, and you can utilize those rods too small to rive. You will need six

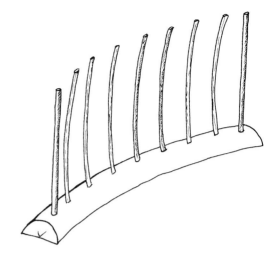

158 *Erect all the zales so they curve the same way as shown*

rods (seven for a ten zale hurdle): four about 2.1m(7ft) long, and two *spur* rods at least 2.7m(9ft) long. These are best woven from the front of the hurdle – that side facing the chopping block.

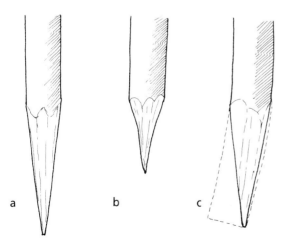

157 *Pointing zales: (a) correct; (b) too short and feathered; (c) how to sharpen a curved butt*

159 *Hurdlemaker picking up the bottom of a sheep hurdle. Note how he ensures the rod bends around the zale, and not vice versa, by working the zale with his left hand*

160 *Picking up the bottom of a hurdle using two* spur
rods (A + B), and four round rods (1–4)

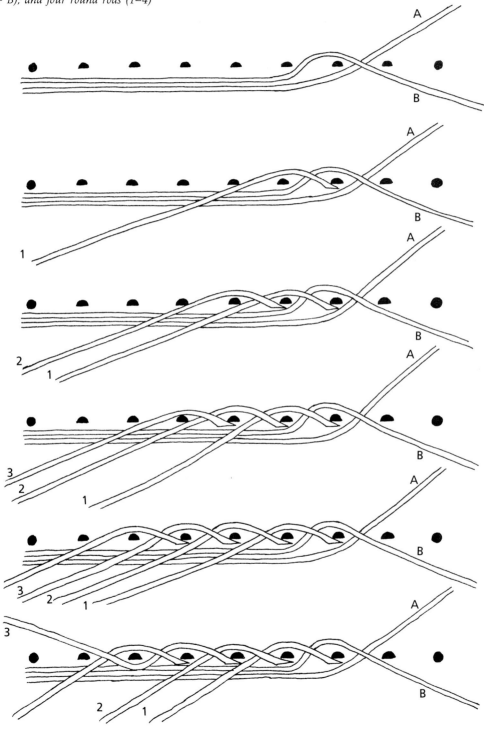

Starting the weave In order to follow the method for picking up the hurdle bottom, read this description in conjunction with figs. 160 and 162. Take the two long spur rods, A and B, and insert them between zales two and three as shown. Leave about 900mm(3ft) of the thin end of each rod beyond the end zale, making sure there are no major knots for the 460mm(18in) beyond that zale or you will be unable to twist the spur rod around it; if there are, re-position the rod to avoid any problem. Now insert the first 2.1m(7ft) rod with its butt in front of zale three as shown. Push it well down to the frame with your foot, holding the zales firmly so that the rod is forced to bend

around them. Repeat this with the three remaining round rods, placing their butts in front of zales four, five and six as shown. (In a ten zale hurdle add one more in front of zale seven). Now, putting your foot on the rods between zales six and seven, carefully lift rod three and take it behind zale eight; do this gently so as not to snap the rod, bending the zale to help. Rods three and four will now extend some 0.9m(3ft) beyond the last zale, and will be used as spur rods similar to A and B. Pick up rod two and weave it to the end of the hurdle, using your feet to push it down, working both the rod and zales so that the former bends around the zales, which are left straight.

Taking rods round the end zale On reaching zale nine, you must take the rod around it and weave it back along the hurdle. To do this without breaking the rod you must first twist

161 Before bending a rod around an end zale, it must be twisted, which this hurdlemaker is just doing, using his foot to stop the rod twisting in the weave

it to separate its fibres: grasp the rod as shown in fig. 161, push it against the zale, and make a large arc with its free end. Once the fibres have parted, twist the rod around the zale, which must be kept vertical to maintain the hurdle's full length. When making sheep hurdles take this rod completely around the zale one extra time.

Filling and tying in the bottom Repeat with rod one what you have just done with two. Now pick up the butt end of spur rod B and weave it to zale nine, leaving any small surplus to be trimmed off. Repeat this with spur rod A. Your hurdle will look as shown in fig. 162, with the weaving higher at zale nine than at zale one. In Dorset and Sussex patterns it is normal to fill in the bottom of the hurdle with round rods; in Hampshire cleft rods are used. Starting at zale six or seven, weave 1.8m(6ft) rods to zale one and back; three or four rods will be sufficient to fill in the base, and once this is level the bottom can be *tied in* using the spur rods.

Carefully pick up spur rod A, bring it to the front of zale one, twist it round that zale, and weave it back into the hurdle. Bring spur rod B to the back of zale one, and repeat. Do the same for spur rods three and four to complete tying in the bottom with a weave which cannot be pulled off.

RAISING THE HURDLE

To *raise* the hurdle you must now work from the back. Start by riving rods about 2.4m(8ft) long, placing their paired clefts on the rod horse ready for use.

Quality of weavers Although you can use your poorer quality rods as *weavers*, certain factors are crucial to making a good hurdle. If you have any thick patches where the split has moved off centre, shave them back to the pith; conversely rods with very thin patches will be no good, so cut these out and use the remaining short lengths to fill up the middle of the hurdle. Make sure you rive between the knots

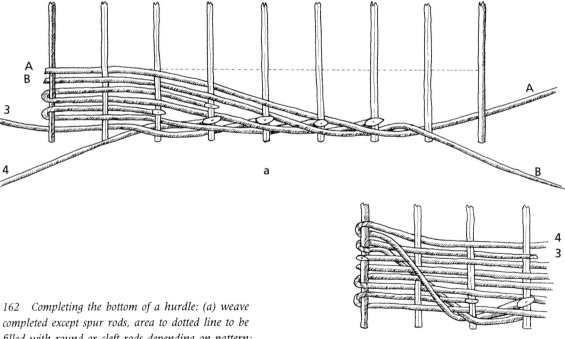

162 *Completing the bottom of a hurdle: (a) weave completed except spur rods, area to dotted line to be filled with round or cleft rods depending on pattern; (b) how spur rods are finished to tie in the bottom*

139

and not through them, as this will reduce the number of badly shaped rods. If your weavers are much thicker than your zales they will distort these when weaving; so quarter the thicker ones and shave off the core, or rive the rod into flat lathes and then use these. Good hurdlemakers waste very little.

Patterns of middle binding   Patterns of *laying in the middle binding* or *heathering* vary. In Dorset and Hampshire weavers are inserted in pairs, two from one end, then two from the other (fig. 163a), and depending on their length some short weavers will be needed to fill the centre of the hurdle and keep the weave level.

In Sussex weavers are laid in quite differently (fig. 163b). Up to six are woven first in one direction and then the other (seven for a

ten zale hurdle), their butt ends being inserted into the already completed weave in the same manner used to secure the top. This system ensures a full centre and a compact, solid weave.

Twilley holes   When making a sheep hurdle, you will remember that a twilley hole is required. Fashion this between the centre two zales when you are about twenty rods up from the frame. Create the gap by using round rods

163   *Patterns for laying in the middle binding:*
(a) Dorset/Hampshire pattern of two paired rods from each end alternately, note the short piece used to fill the middle; (b) Sussex pattern of up to six rods from each side alternately

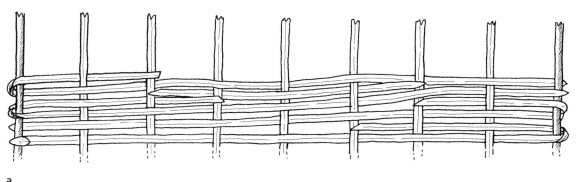

a

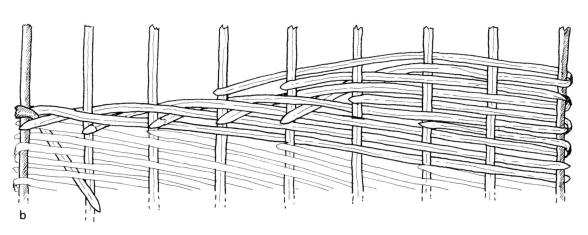

b

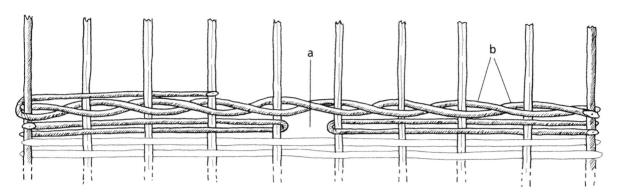

164 A twilley hole: use round rods to make a gap (a), and two twilley rods (b) above it to keep the zales straight

which you must bring back to the ends of the hurdle by twisting them around zales five and six (fig. 164). Above these you must interweave two *twilley rods* running the full width of the hurdle to keep the zales straight and provide a smooth surface with which to carry the hurdle. In a Dorset hurdle (fig. 153a) no rods are twisted around zale five, allowing the twilley hole to extend towards zale one.

If you make a lamb creep hurdle, leave a gap about ten weavers in depth (fig. 153c).

Laying in the weavers   There are some basic rules you must follow when *laying in* weavers if you are to make a strong flat hurdle free from unplanned holes. Always lay in the butt end first, with its riven face to the front of the hurdle. If a rod has any bad knots, note where they fall: if it is where you need to twist the rod or where it will break around a zale, move it along to avoid the problem, because it is better to lose a few inches from the butt than to lose a whole rod. Never start weaving on one side of a zale if a rod has finished on its other side (fig. 165a), rather start the new weaver on the same side. Do not finish two weavers together on the same side of a zale (fig. 165b), or you will create a gap.

Whilst weaving you must continually *work* the hurdle: push the rods down with your feet,

your knees, and when too high for this, your mallet; work the zales to and fro to pinch and push the rods down, never open them up to let the rod drop; always flex the weavers around the zales, which should be held firmly when you are pushing weavers down so it is these that bend and not the zales. At all times you must aim to keep the zales straight and the weave flat and even. If you have a weaver which is too thick, try twisting it to make it more flexible, or if this fails, nick it at the back with your hook so that it will bend where required.

If, despite all your working, your hurdle

165 Weaving faults: (a) do not start and finish weavers on opposite sides of the inner zales, start them on the same side; (b) finishing two weavers at the same zale will create a gap in the weave

a

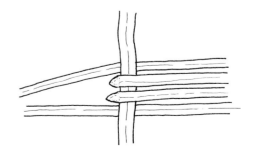

b

141

does start becoming 'S' shaped, it can usually be straightened by using two *twilley* rods. These round rods are stiffer than clefts, and when heathered across the hurdle (fig. 167), will help to bring errant zales into line.

'Look after the middle and the ends will look after themselves' is the rule to abide by. As you weave, make sure the middle is kept *full*, not lower than either end. Short part-rods can be inserted to achieve this, and if you go too far it is possible to cut a rod out four or five below the top and force the weave down in order to fit your finishing rods.

Turning weavers around zales As you raise the hurdle it will be necessary to turn longer weavers around both end zales in order to tie the hurdle together. To do this you must twist the weaver.

If it is in front of the zale (remember you are working from the back), pull it against this and twist it upwards and towards yourself (fig.

166). Work the weaver up and down to extend the separated fibres, and then bring it close around the zale. If the weaver is behind the zale, again push it hard against this and twist downwards and away from you, using the same method to loosen the fibres and turn it neatly close around the zale. Use the hurdle gauge stick regularly to ensure that you are not pulling the end zales inwards as you work up the hurdle (fig. 168). It will take some practice to master this technique, but your wood must be green and supple: if you have not made your hurdles by the end of May at the latest, it will probably be too dry.

SECURING THE TOP BINDING

As with picking up the bottom, there is a standard pattern to the top weave designed to give a tight finish that is secure when in use.

As you complete laying in the body of the hurdle, aim to finish the weave about 75mm

166 *Turning a weaver: (a) pull against the zale and twist; (b) remember if weaver in front of zale twist towards you (x), if behind zale, twist away (y)*

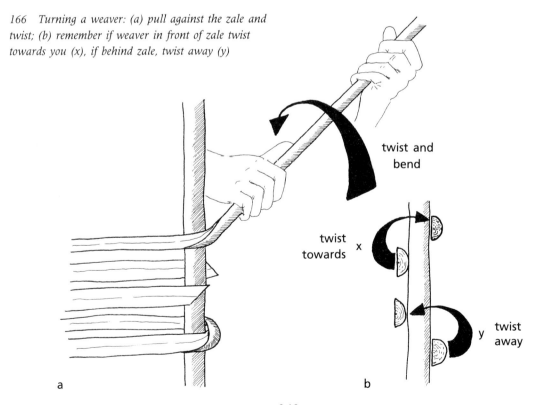

twist and bend

twist towards x

twist away y

a

b

(3in) below zale nine (your right hand side working from behind the hurdle), and about 200mm(8in) below zale one. You should now follow this description of finishing in conjunction with fig. 169.

You will need four cleft weavers 1.8 to 2.4m(6 to 8ft) long (five for a ten zale hurdle), and two round rods called the *stump rod* 1.2m(4ft) and the *finishing rod* 2.4m(8ft).

Thrust the butt end of the first weaver, called the *spur*, down into the weave so it emerges in front of zale eight about 230mm (9in) down; bend it gently so it comes in front of zale nine, twist it around the zale and weave normally. Take the *first top weaver*, insert it in front of zale nine and below the spur, and then weave normally. Push the *second top weaver* in front of zale eight, underneath both spur and first top weaver, then weave. Repeat as shown for the *third top weaver*. Now insert the round stump rod in front of zale six, beneath the second and third weavers, weave it to zale one, but do not bring it behind it at this stage. Start the very last rod, the finishing rod, in front of zale five as shown; weave to zale one where you must twist it and wind it around this zale twice; bend it back along the top, cut off any surplus extending beyond zale four, and then force the end into the weave so it finishes in front of zale four as shown. Grip the finishing rod and lever it up and over zale two. Finally pick up the end of the stump rod and bring it behind zale one and over the finishing rod.

FINISHING OFF

Trimming Use a nug-axe or the straight edge of a hurdling bill to trim the surplus from any weavers protruding beyond either end zale. Then trim the face of the hurdle so that no weavers extend beyond a zale. Be very careful not to cut through any adjacent weavers, and although good hurdlemakers can cut them in-situ using a nug-axe, it is safer to lift the end of each weaver with a piece of waste wood and then cut the surplus *noggin* off (fig. 170). Similarly trim back any surplus from the top of

167 Two round twilley rods being pushed into place. Hurdlemakers use their hands, knees and feet to push weavers into place

168 A hurdlemaker using his measuring stick to ensure the end zales are not being pulled in. Note the nug-axe in his other hand

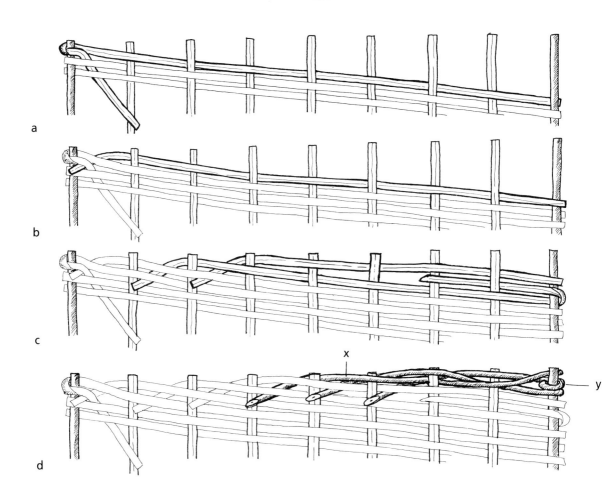

a

b

c

d

x

y

*169 Securing the top binding: (a) spur inserted;
(b) first top weaver in place; (c) second and third top
weavers in place; (d) stump rod (x) and finishing rod
(y) in place; (e-h) detail of weaving stump and finishing
rods*

the zales to leave them 25mm(1in) above the weave.

A sharp kick at either end of the frame should loosen the hurdle sufficiently to remove it, but if it does stick, carefully lever it out with a rod. Some hurdlemakers remove their hurdles before trimming, preferring to perform this job with the hurdle resting against their stomach, and you may find this easier. If you make a 1.8m(6ft) screen you will have to re-move it from the frame at 1.2m(4ft) or so, trim

it, and then lean it against your rod horse in order to both finish and trim the top portion.

Storage Store your hurdles flat, one on top of the other, the lowest held off the ground by poles. Place them front (or cleft face) down so the weight of the pile tends to flatten them. Do not cover the sides of your stack, but allow the air to get through it to dry and tighten the weave.

Shackles and shores As we have seen, sheep hurdles need supporting to make a secure fold, and it is the hurdlemaker's job to provide the sharpened stakes or *shores* for driving into the ground in order to do this. *Shackles* are loops of twisted hazel, about 260mm(10in) diameter

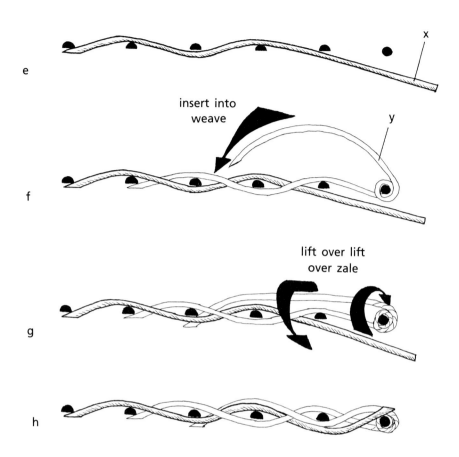

e

insert into
weave

y

f

lift over lift
over zale

g

h

that can be pushed over the end zales of two adjacent hurdles and a shore to bind all three together.

With any luck you will now have made your first hurdle. It probably took a long time, made your hands sore, and contained many faults! But remember an average hurdle may contain up to 60 pieces of wood, all slightly different in shape and texture. It is not surprising that one hurdlemaker told me that in 40 years he had never made a hurdle that he could not criticize in some way!

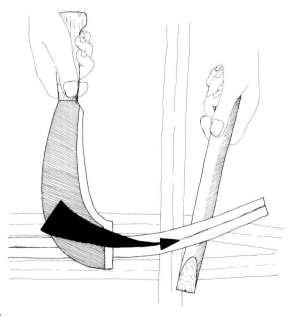

170   To trim the finished hurdle, use a piece of waste wood to lift each weaver clear before cutting with a nug-axe or handbill (shown)

CHAPTER · FOURTEEN

Modern Markets and Their Economics

'Stop telling me to manage my woods . . . please, no more conservationists expounding the merits of coppicing . . . until someone shows me how to sell wood without making a thumping great loss'. These words, quoted by The Anglican Woodland Project Direction, Vincent Thurkettle, sum up the dilemma faced by many woodland owners. When thatchers travel hundreds of miles to purchase their hazel wood, when gardeners wait 18 months for their wattle screens, and when 95 per cent of the charcoal consumed in England is imported, it is hard to believe.

In truth there is as yet no convincing answer to that owner's problem. Those with the right wood in the right condition can make a satisfactory return; those without cannot. But new approaches to coppice, blending traditional with new markets, are turning the tide of neglect, and every woodman, owner and manager should keep abreast of these changes that are gradually re-kindling underwood industries in several countries. Remember that although this chapter explores the established markets, the scope is almost endless, ranging from long straight poles for tepees to dogwood twigs used as the decorative stalks of turnery fruits.

The Market for Coppice Today

TRADITIONAL PRODUCTS

Wattle hurdles Sheep hurdles enjoy a very small market today. The growing practice of lambing indoors has seen to that. But some shepherds continue to fold their ewes in the traditional manner, creating sales for perhaps 1000 each year.

Garden screening on the other hand is a growing market. Over 25,000 wattle screens are sold every year, a figure which has doubled in the last thirty years, and is continuing to grow. Demand far exceeds the supply of suitable hazel from which to make them, most customers having to wait up to 18 months. Made in sizes from 900mm(3ft) to 1.8m(6ft) high, they are priced per 300mm(1ft) of height; and it is the taller more expensive screens that account for more than half of annual sales. Willow, once commonly used in Europe for wattles, is being used by some hurdle makers in place of hazel, but it has a poorer reputation for durability.

Thatching wood It is estimated that England has over 1,000 thatchers who every year repair

4,500 ridges, and re-cover 2,000 thatched buildings. Since each roof uses between six and twelve thousand hazel broches, the market for these is enormous, possibly 20 million per annum, which at current prices makes it a million pound market! Fortunately plastic alternatives have so far proven unsatisfactory. Remember round wood can be sold to broche makers as well as thatchers.

Gate hurdles As with wattle sheep hurdles, this is now a small market of perhaps 1,000 a year, mainly to regular customers, and more often in chestnut than in ash wood.

Chestnut fencing This remains an important industry in southern England, where more than half the coppices are of chestnut. Spile or stake makers still find demand sufficient to make a living, but more important is the cleft pale and wire product. Made to a British Standard, it is supported by its own organization, the Chestnut Fencing Manufacturers Society, which can be contacted through the Rural Development Commission.

A more limited market for three year rotation chestnut exists in the manufacture of walking sticks for hospital use, again to a British Standard specification.

For gardens and hedges For those prepared to get out and sell, these smaller markets still thrive on a local basis. Good bean rods, peasticks and flower stakes can all be sold directly to local customers. Hedge laying now attracts grants in some areas, so stakes and binders are once again it demand.

Faggots Whilst true faggots are no longer purchased for firing ovens, their 2.5m(8ft) long brethren used in river defence work are. In eastern England 20,000 are purchased annually by the regional water authority. These bundles of 25 rods sell for about half the value of thatching wood. And if, in desperation, you do burn the brash, keep the ash and sell it to potters.

Odds and ends There are a few specialized markets that can repay investigating. Any unusual woods or particularly fine butts are always worth offering to local turners or furniture makers, some of whom specialize in using round wood. Pole lathe turning is a craft rapidly regaining popularity on both sides of the Atlantic. It has an active association, and contact with this and other craft schools may provide a small market. And keep your eye open for niche markets like the morris dancers who find coppice poles cheaper and more expendable than shop-bought pick-axe handles.

GENERAL MARKETS FOR BULK WOOD

Today many coppices contain wood beyond its optimum age for use by craftsmen, but for which there are markets. These are essential to anyone restoring a neglected woodland, and can be identified with the help of the state forestry service.

Turnery Every year in southern England over 15,000 tons of poles go to rural factories making brooms and brush heads. Each turnery will have its own, usually undemanding specification.

Pulp and board mills With the major mill recently converted to re-cycling paper, only two mills in England still handle logwood. This means a long haul for many owners, but is worth considering when cutting large acreages of long rotation coppice.

Firewood After the great storm of 1987, it seemed that everyone acquired a chainsaw and cut their own. Now the market has returned to some normality, firewood can be sold in the cord direct from the wood, as logs delivered in bulk, or as logs in plastic sacks. The increasing use of wood burning stoves for heating and cooking, a tradition stronger in America and Europe than in England, offers some security to future sales.

Charcoal In 1991 60,000 tons of charcoal were sold in Britain. Unfortunately only five per cent of this growing market was home produced, providing a use for only 500 acres of woodland. Over half of these sales occur during a short summer period when barbecues are in use; 3kg(6.6lbs) bags are the most popular retail pack (fig. 174). The balance is used for industrial processes such as metal refining.

Woodchips Modern tractor-powered machinery can reduce a pole to a pile of woodchips in no time. The search for renewable energy sources has focused on this material, and heating plants both domestic and industrial are already operating in Scandinavia and England. The Department of Energy is now funding research which could make this a market of the future for otherwise uneconomic coppice.

THE ECONOMICS OF COPPICING

Although the price of an individual commodity often appears very attractive, the actual profit achieved from its production can vary enormously depending on the yield, age of crop and labour cost. The following examples are based on results currently being achieved in some English coppices.

HAZEL COPPICE

Together with chestnut, hazel is the most profitable coppice crop, currently enjoying an increasing demand and a shortage of suitable raw material.

One acre of well-stocked hazel will produce 10–12,000 rods, or 400 bundles of 25 each. About three quarters of these can be sold for thatching, with the balance going as bean rods, pea-sticks etc. After deducting the cost of buying an acre of standing wood, a return of £1,500 per acre should result.

You can of course add value to these rods in the wood. From 400 bundles of rods you can make roughly 75,000 broches, which together with pea and bean sticks will raise your return to £5,250 per acre before labour. A fur-

ther step is to make wattle garden screens, of which some 300 1.8m(6ft) examples can be made from the 400 bundles of rods, further increasing your return to £6,300 per acre.

Although the return per acre from broche and hurdle making is considerably more than from selling rods, this difference reflects the much longer time required to make them. It takes only one week to fell an acre of hazel, but four weeks to sort and bundle it, and eight weeks to make 300 screens. It pays to make broches or screens if you can make them efficiently, and good hurdlemakers make a comfortable living.

MIXED COPPICE

There are over 30,000 acres of mixed coppice in England. Financial returns vary depending on its age and marketability (fig. 171).

Much of it has not been cut for 40 or 50 years, at which age it is suitable only for firewood, although particularly good butts of ash or maple are saleable to furniture makers or turners. Forty year-old coppice should produce 25–30 tons of firewood per acre plus a few hundred stakes, giving a return of £840, which can be raised to £1,400 by logging and delivering the firewood.

At about 17 years old, this same coppice will produce stakes or handles (appendix 3) which given a suitable market, will sell for about £600 per acre. Although this is less than firewood, twice the acreage can be cut with the same labour.

Much mixed coppice is rich in hazel, so when young it can be cut to utilize this wood for thatching. At ten years it should produce up to 9,000 rods per acre, and a return of £1,200 per acre without adding any value by further

171 (Right) *How the profitability of mixed coppice varies with age, assuming approximately 40 per cent is hazel. (a) shows the relative percentage of craft material (—) and firewood (+); (b) the value per acre; and (c) the value per acre per year*

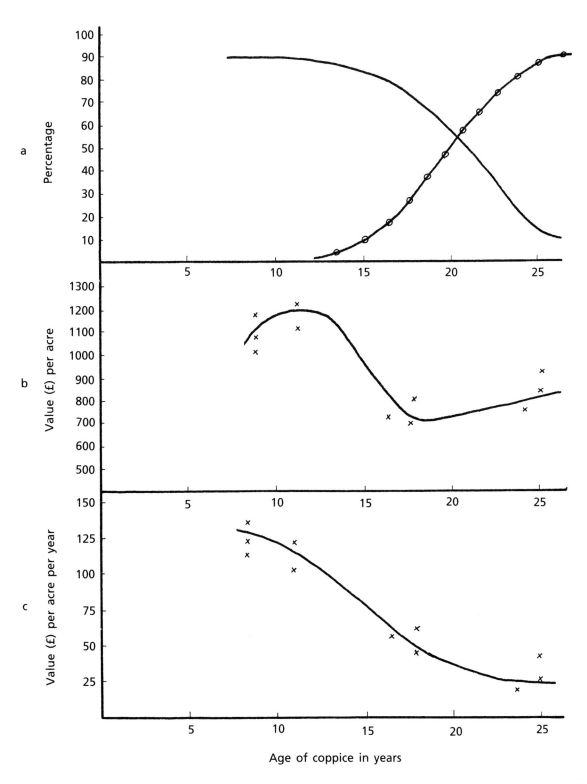

Age of coppice in years

conversion. As the graphs in fig. 171 show, coppice cut young produces more material for craft use than old coppice, but most importantly gives five or six times the return per acre per year because four or five crops of rods can be harvested in the time taken to produce one crop of firewood. Unfortunately market forces will usually determine whether you can cut at the optimum age.

CHARCOAL

Converting wood into charcoal which, despite losing 80 per cent of its weight in the process, is increased in value five times, would seem good business. But the traditional method using an earth clamp is very dirty work and requires very unsocial working hours. Portable steel kilns (fig. 172) are less demanding, but they require a capital investment.

Charcoal is best produced from 20 year old coppice, and because re-siting the kilns is a time-consuming business, it should be done on a site with plenty of seasoned cord-wood available. Two kilns are best, since one can be loading or unloading whilst the other is burning and cooling, a process taking approximately 72 hours. Two kilns should produce 12 burns per month and about 4.5 tons of charcoal, which has to be sieved, graded, weighed and bagged for sale. The New Woodmanship Trust, who have carried out a pilot project, estimate the net return towards labour over a full year using this system would be about £8,000, with the collier working a 60 hour week. Charcoal burning on this scale is best integrated into the overall management of a woodland, using up only wood that cannot be profitably sold, whilst the woodman pursues other crafts with the valuable material. A simple method using oil drums (Appendix Four) offers scope for small scale operations or test marketing the product.

On a larger scale charcoal can be produced in fixed site wood distillation plants, where the intention is also to collect the valuable by-products, mainly naphtha, acetic acid and wood tar. Large plants of this type may have an es-

sential role in the future preservation of large acreages of coppice woodland in southern England.

GRANT AID

Grants and subsidies are the tools with which bureaucrats fashion their current policies. They have a sad history. They led to the coniferization of many broad leaved woodlands, the grubbing out of others, and a surfeit of unnecessary planting. A new awareness of the irreplaceable heritage our woodlands represent has remedied this, and owners should take advantage of the grants available for restoring native woodlands (fig. 173).

Woodland grant scheme   The latest scheme from the Forestry Authority offers financial assistance for those undertaking uneconomic coppicing. In order to qualify an owner has to produce both a 30 year strategy and a work plan for his woodland, based on maintaining and enhancing

172   *A modern charcoal kiln is basically one or more stackable steel rings with a lid on the top. Four chimneys arise from the base, where there are also air inlets (centre). A one ring kiln can produce 272kg(900lbs) of charcoal in 72 hours*

173 Literature explaining some of the grants and marketing initiatives available to woodland owners

MARKETING SMALL WOOD

LOCAL MARKETS, DIRECT TO THE CUSTOMER

Most coppice products have customarily attracted low prices, leaving little margin for woodmen supplying solely wholesalers. They preferred to sell the bulk of their products direct to local customers. It remains true today that greater returns come from selling direct: a retailer's mark-up on charcoal, for instance, is 100 per cent. Try to develop a core of regular customers you know will purchase a certain quantity every year. Consistent quality is essential because the best advertising comes from satisfied customers; if your price and quality are right, then new customers will seek you out.

An excellent way to make direct contact with customers is to organize a display at craft fairs or county shows. Demonstrations of craft work are popular with those attending, frequently attract orders, and provide trade or conservation bodies with the opportunity to inform a wider public about themselves.

ORGANIZED MARKETING

Each craftsman supplying his local market has clear benefits, but we have seen that in the past this isolation, lack of organization, and lack of capital to exploit new markets all contributed to the rapid decline of the underwood trades. The first steps have already been taken to ensure this error is not repeated.

The chestnut fencing industry now has its own trade association; several County Councils are encouraging the re-instatement of coppice woodlands; The Anglian Woodland Project, a partnership between Forestry Authority, Countryside Commission and County Councils, is active in developing marketing opportunities for small woodlands; and The Coppice Association has been formed to act as the representative body for the coppice industry. No one involved in woodland crafts should fail to take

its ecosystems, aesthetic value and genetic integrity, whilst producing utilizable wood. A grant is then available for the whole acreage to be brought under management.

Local authorities Some local authorities offer grants to owners carrying out the initial coppicing of neglected woodland. Depending on the particular area, these may be related to landscape value or targeted at certain species. For example Hampshire County Council offers grants for restoring hazel coppice that amount to half of the total cost.

Other sources A significant number of ancient woodlands are now either nature reserves, publicly owned, or have been designated as Sites of Special Scientific Interest by English Nature. Sites falling into these categories may attract management grants from governmental bodies, charities, or even private companies funding conservation work as a part of their public relations programme. Conservationists are well aware of these sources, but the uninitiated should beware of imposed conditions that may restrict effective management.

advantage of these initiatives.

Today's coppice worker or manager must be marketing man as well as craftsman (fig. 174). It is no longer sufficient merely to produce products in the hope that someone will buy them; they have to be tailored to the customer's needs. How to go about this is illustrated by the example of staves for morris dancers. It was noticed that many groups of morris dancers consume a considerable number of staves each year. The main source of these was pick-axe handles, which were both expensive and splintered badly in use. New staves were made from straight coppice poles of ash which did not splinter as much. Value was added to these simple poles by rinding and smoothing them, and cutting them exactly the size required. The cost of the raw material, labour to fell and prepare them, together with a good profit margin, was found to be less than a pick-axe handle. Finally, using the image of a better quality traditional product, the new stave was promoted by contacting local morris dancing groups and showing them samples. Regular, profitable orders resulted.

COMMERCE VERSUS CONSERVATION

Some people perceive a conflict between woodmanship and nature conservation: to them felling trees is the antithesis of conserving. Certainly if there remained in England any primeval forest it would be a travesty to subject it to either felling or the modern passion for tidiness. But that is not the case; our woodlands all result from man's interference and the harsh reality is that without their valuable products even fewer would have survived.

Coppicing is an example of man working with nature, intent on preserving woodlands and their trees. The results are as important for conservationists as for woodmen: because there is no need for planting, each woodland retains its genetic individuality; a variety of habitats results from the different aged cants, each attracting its own special fauna, some releasing breathtaking displays of vernal flowers as the shade is briefly removed; and gnarled, hollow stools of remarkable ages provide home to lichens, mosses and small mammals. If you need convincing, visit Bradfield Woods, near Bury St. Edmunds in Suffolk, and experience a woodland coppiced continuously for over 800 years, and arguably now the richest and most beautiful in England.

To retain this balance, never let commercial need override good practice. If you manage a nature reserve, work out the optimum rotations for both financial return and wildlife interest. Like hazel they may co-incide, but if not, find a compromise: let neither rule the roost. Remember the lesson of Bradfield: steady sales support the continuous management needed to maintain the rich diversity of an ancient coppice.

174 Strong marketing direct to the customer is crucial. This charcoal, made on the Isle of Wight, sells well with its clear message about saving woodlands

APPENDICES

APPENDIX ONE

DIMENSIONS OF LESS COMMON TOOLS

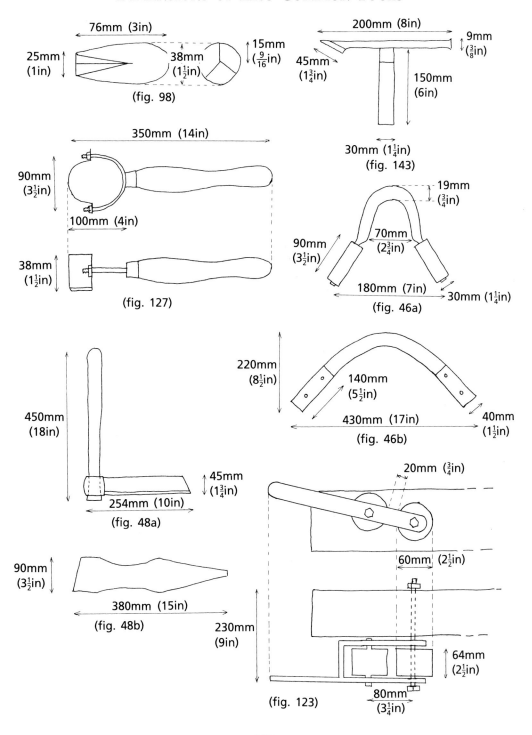

76mm (3in)

25mm (1in)

38mm (1½in)

15mm (⁹⁄₁₆in)

(fig. 98)

200mm (8in)

9mm (⅜in)

45mm (1¾in)

150mm (6in)

30mm (1¼in)

(fig. 143)

350mm (14in)

90mm (3½in)

100mm (4in)

38mm (1½in)

(fig. 127)

19mm (¾in)

90mm (3½in)

70mm (2¾in)

180mm (7in)

30mm (1¼in)

(fig. 46a)

220mm (8½in)

140mm (5½in)

430mm (17in)

40mm (1½in)

(fig. 46b)

450mm (18in)

45mm (1¾in)

254mm (10in)

(fig. 48a)

90mm (3½in)

380mm (15in)

(fig. 48b)

20mm (¾in)

60mm (2½in)

230mm (9in)

64mm (2½in)

80mm (3¼in)

(fig. 123)

APPENDIX TWO
DIMENSIONS OF WOODMAN'S DEVICES

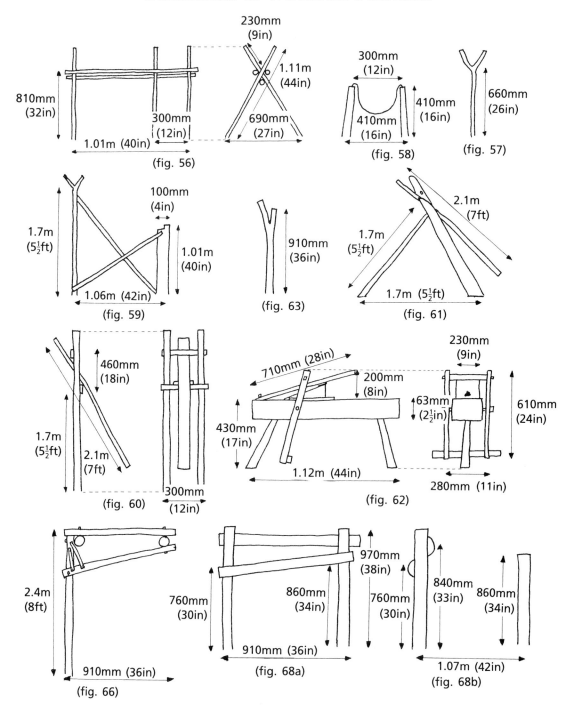

230mm (9in)

1.11m (44in)

690mm (27in)

810mm (32in)

300mm (12in)

1.01m (40in)

(fig. 56)

300mm (12in)

410mm (16in)

410mm (16in)

(fig. 58)

660mm (26in)

(fig. 57)

100mm (4in)

1.7m (5½ft)

1.01m (40in)

1.06m (42in)

(fig. 59)

910mm (36in)

(fig. 63)

2.1m (7ft)

1.7m (5½ft)

1.7m (5½ft)

(fig. 61)

460mm (18in)

710mm (28in)

200mm (8in)

230mm (9in)

63mm (2½in)

610mm (24in)

1.7m (5½ft)

2.1m (7ft)

430mm (17in)

1.12m (44in)

280mm (11in)

(fig. 62)

300mm (12in)

(fig. 60)

2.4m (8ft)

910mm (36in)

(fig. 66)

760mm (30in)

860mm (34in)

970mm (38in)

760mm (30in)

910mm (36in)

(fig. 68a)

840mm (33in)

860mm (34in)

1.07m (42in)

(fig. 68b)

APPENDIX THREE
USEFUL MEASURES

ENGLISH MEASURES OF LENGTH AND AREA

1 in		=	25mm		
1 ft	= 12in	=	0.3m	=	300mm
1 yard	= 3ft	=	0.91m		
1 chain	= 22yds	=	20m		
1 acre	= 10sq chains	=	4840 sq yds	=	0.4hectare

ENGLISH MEASURES OF VOLUME AND WEIGHT

1 cord is 8 × 4 × 4ft		=	2.4 × 1.2 × 1.2m
or 16 × 4 × 2ft		=	4.9 × 1.2 × 0.6m
= 128 cu ft		=	3.62cu m
1 cu ft hardwood	= 43.75lb	=	19.85kg/.028cu m
1 cord (50% air)	= 2800lb	=	1270kg
1 ton	= 2240lb	=	1.016 tonne
1 cord	= 1.25ton	=	1.27 tonne

NUMBER OF STOOLS TO THE ACRE

Spacing	m	1.52	1.83	2.13	2.44	3.05	4.57	6.1
	ft	5	6	7	8	10	15	20
Number per acre		1742	1210	889	680	435	193	108

YIELDS (The following figures are a guide only)

Species	stools/acre	rods/acre	product/acre
Hazel in rotation* (9 yrs old)	600	11,000	300 wattles + 250 bundles pea sticks + 10 bundles bean rods or 500 bundles thatching rods
Unworked hazel (19 yrs old)	400	4,500	no wattles + 60 bundles pea sticks + 80 bundles thatching rods + 1000 stakes + 2 cords
Chestnut in rotation** (16 years old)	590	2,350	603 bundles pales + 1500 stakes + 30 bundles pea sticks + $6\frac{1}{2}$ cords (app 8 tons)
Mixed coppice (50 yrs old)	320	2,620	150 stakes + 15 bundles thatching rods + 24 cords (app 30 tons)
Mixed coppice (17 yrs old)	440	3,600	800 stakes + 60 bundles thatching rods + 30 bundles pea sticks + 4 cords (app 6 tons)

* Anon, *Utilization of Hazel Coppice*, Forestry Commission Bulletin No. 27, 1956
* Jonathan Howe, *Hazel Coppice, The Hampshire Experience*, Hampshire County Council, 1991
** C.D. Begley, *Growth and Yield of Sweet Chestnut Coppice*, Forestry Commission Forest Record No. 30, 1955

APPENDIX FOUR
MAKING CHARCOAL IN A STEEL DRUM (see fig. 175)

This simple process requires no capital, takes very little time, can be easily stopped, and requires minimal supervision. It is ideal for anyone with small amounts of waste wood not easily saleable as firewood.

1 Using a cold chisel prepare the drum by making five 50mm(2in) holes in one end, and completely removing the other. Knock up the cut edge of the open end to form a ledge.

2 Position the drum, open end upwards, on three bricks to allow an air flow to the five holes in the base.

3 Place paper, kindling and brown ends (incompletely charred butts from the last burn) into the bottom of the drum, and light.

4 Once it is burning well, load branchwood, at random to allow air spaces, until the drum is completely full. Keep the pieces to a fairly even diameter, but put any larger ones towards the bottom where they will be subject to longer charring.

5 When the fire is hot and clearly will not go out, restrict air access around the base by using soil piled against it, but leaving one 100mm(4in) gap. Also place the lid on top, leaving a *small* gap at one side for smoke to exit.

6 Dense white *wet* smoke will issue during the charring process. When this visibly slows, bang the drum to settle the wood down, creating more white smoke.

7 When the smoke turns from white (mainly water being driven off) to thin blue (charcoal starting to burn), stop the burn by firstly closing off *all* air access to the base using more earth, and secondly placing the top lid firmly on its ledge, making it airtight by the addition of sods and soil as required. The burn will take between three and four hours.

8 After cooling for about 24 hours, the drum can be tipped over, the charcoal emptied on to a sheet, and graded and packed.

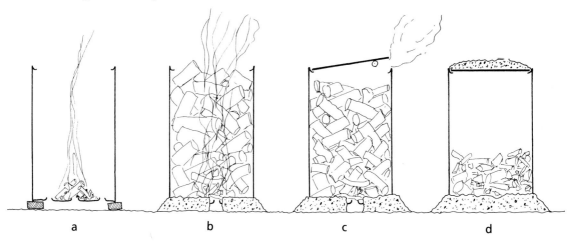

175 *Making charcoal in a drum: (a) starting the fire; (b) adding the wood; (c) stopping down the fire with earth at the base, and lid on top; (d) stopping the burn when charring finished by excluding* all *air*

BIBLIOGRAPHY

M. ABBOTT *Green woodwork – working with wood the natural way*, Guild of Master Craftsman Publications, 1989

ANON. *Utilization of hazel coppice*, Forestry Commission Bulletin No. 27, HMSO, 1956

C. BEGLEY *Growth and yield of sweet chestnut coppice*, Forestry Commission Forest Record No. 30, HMSO, 1955

A. BROOKS *The Power Chain Saw*, British Trust for Conservation Volunteers, 1974

J. BROWN *The Forester*, Blackwood, 1882

N. DANNATT *Marketing of coppice and other small roundwood in South East England*, Kent County Council, 1992

H. EDLIN *Woodland Crafts in Britain*, Batsford, 1949

J. EVELYN *Sylva, or a discourse on forest trees*, lst Edition London, 1664 and ed. J. Hunter, London, 1786

H. FITZRANDOLPH and M. HAY *The rural industries of England and Wales Volume 1*, OUP, 1926

J. HOWE *Hazel coppice – past present and future*, Hampshire County Council, 1991

D. LANGSNER *Country Woodcraft*, Rodale Press, 1978

W. LLOYD *Lakeland Charcoal, a report from the New Woodmanship Trust to the Lake District National Park*, 1987

J. NISBET English coppices and copsewoods in *Journals of the Board of Agriculture*, pp293–305 and 479–488, 1902

G. PETERKEN *Woodland Conservation and Management*, Chapman & Hall, 1981

O. RACKHAM *Ancient woodland – its history, vegetation and uses in England*, Arnold, 1980

R. TABOR English billhook patterns in *Tool and Trades History Society Newsletter* No. 11, 1985

R. TABOR A role for hazel in woodland conservation in *Quarterly Journal of Forestry* Vol LXXXIII, pp177–182, 1989

R. UNDERHILL *The Woodwright's Shop*, and *The Woodwright's Companion*, University of North Carolina Press, 1981 and 1983

K. S. WOODS *Rural Crafts of England*, Harrap, 1949

USEFUL ADDRESSES

SOURCES OF AND INFORMATION ABOUT TOOLS

Andrew Breese, Chalk Pits Forge, Chalk Pits Museum, Houghton Bridge, Amberley, West Sussex BN18 9LT

Grange Farm Recycled Tools, Bradcar Lane, Shropham, Norfolk

Alec Morris, The Iron Mills, Dunsford, Nr. Exeter, Devon

The Tool and Trades History Society, 60 Swanley Lane, Swanley, Kent BR8 7JG

Visa Hand Tools Ltd., Unit 3, Tweed Road Industrial Estate, Clevedon, Bristol BS21 6RR

WOODLAND ORGANIZATIONS

Anglian Woodland Project, Forest Office, Santon Downham, Brandon, Suffolk IP27 OTJ

The Coppice Association, Eastern Cottage, Main Road, Toft, near Bourne, Lincolnshire PE10 OJT

The Forestry Commission, 231 Corstorphine Road, Edinburgh EH12 7AT

The National Trust, 36 Queen Anne's Gate, London SW1H 9AS

The Royal Forestry Society, 102 High Street, Tring, Hertfordshire HP23 4AF

Royal Society for Nature Conservation (The Wildlife Trusts Partnership), The Green, Witham Park, Waterside South, Lincoln LN5 7JR

The Woodland Trust, Autumn Park, Grantham, Lincolnshire NG31 6LL

ORGANIZATIONS RUNNING COURSES

Anglesey Chair Bodgers, Hen Felin Wen, Dwyran, Anglesey LL61 6AQ

British Trust for Conservation Volunteers, 36 St. Mary's Street, Wallingford, Oxfordshire OX10 OEU

Brotus Rural Craft Centre (Ken Grieve), Newhall Farm, Burnturk, Ladybank, Fife KY7 7TR

Centre for Alternative Technology, Machynlleth, Powys SY20 9AZ

The Coppice Association (Richard Edwards), Eastern Cottage, Main Road, Toft, near Bourne, Lincolnshire PO10 0JT

Country Workshops, 90 Mill Creek Road, Marshall, NC 28753 USA

The Green Wood Trust, Station Road, Coalbrookdale, Telford, Shropshire TF8 7DR

Handcraft Woodworks, PO Box 1322, Mendocino, Ca 95460 USA

Hay Bridge Nature Reserve (Anne Frahm), Low Hay Bridge, Bouth, Ulverston, Cumbria LA12 8JG

Living Wood Training, 159 Cotswold Road, Windmill Hill, Bristol BS3 4PH

School for Woodland Industries, Hooke Park, Parnham House, Beaminster, Dorset DT8 3NA

OTHER USEFUL ADDRESSES

The Association of Pole Lathe Turners, 159 Cotswold Road, Windmill Hill, Bristol BS3 4PH

Farming and Wildlife Advisory Group, National Agricultural Centre, Stoneleigh, Kenilworth, Warwickshire CV8 2RX

Rural Development Commission, 141 Castle Street, Salisbury, Wiltshire SP1 3TP

INDEX